Windows Phon
Made Simple

Jon Westfall

Apress®

Windows Phone 7 Made Simple

ISBN-13 (pbk): 978-1-4302-3312-1

ISBN-13 (electronic): 978-1-4302-3313-8

Printed and bound in the United States of America (POD)

President and Publisher: Paul Manning
Lead Editor: Mark Beckner
Developmental Editor: James Markham
Technical Reviewer: Steven Hughes
Editorial Board: Steve Anglin, Mark Beckner, Ewan Buckingham, Gary Cornell, Jonathan Gennick, Jonathan Hassell, Michelle Lowman, Matthew Moodie, Jeffrey Pepper, Frank Pohlmann, Douglas Pundick, Ben Renow-Clarke, Dominic Shakeshaft, Matt Wade, Tom Welsh
Coordinating Editor: Kelly Moritz
Copy Editor: Mary Ann Fugate, Patrick Meador
Compositor: MacPS, LLC
Indexer: BIM Indexing & Proofreading Services
Cover Designer: Anna Ishchenko

Distributed to the book trade worldwide by Springer Science+Business Media, LLC., 233 Spring Street, 6th Floor, New York, NY 10013. Phone 1-800-SPRINGER, fax (201) 348-4505, e-mail orders-ny@springer-sbm.com, or visit www.springeronline.com.

For information on translations, please e-mail rights@apress.com, or visit www.apress.com.

Apress and friends of ED books may be purchased in bulk for academic, corporate, or promotional use. eBook versions and licenses are also available for most titles. For more information, reference our Special Bulk Sales–eBook Licensing web page at www.apress.com/info/bulksales.

Dedicated to my family, friends, mentors, and students

Contents at a Glance

Contents

About the Author

 **Jon Westfall** is not easily categorized. Working as a programmer, system administrator, and consultant for over 15 years, Jon has acquired an interesting skill set that he uses not only in the area of Information Technology, but also as an experimental psychologist studying how humans make decisions. Jon currently writes for the Thoughts Media network, serving as News Editor of Windows Phone Thoughts (www.windowsphonethoughts.com) and Executive Editor of Android Thoughts (www.androidthoughts.com). He holds a Ph.D. in Cognitive Experimental Psychology, and is recognized by Microsoft as a Most Valuable Professional for Windows Phone.

This is his second book. Previously he has written a novel, *Mandate* (www.getmandate.com), and maintains a personal blog at jonwestfall.com. He can be contacted at jon@jonwestfall.com, or on Twitter, (@jonwestfall).

About the Technical Reviewer

**Steven Hughes** has been a Microsoft Windows Phone MVP for the past decade for his passion and dedication in the mobile community. Steven became involved with handheld computers since the early '90s including the beta testing and the prototype design of several hardware and software designs. His passion and knowledge of mobile technology and the mobile industry has advised and consulted many on its use and has earned the nickname 'fyiguy' as result. Steven loves to share information and help people; you may see his contributions and articles on several websites, publications, podcasts, and other productions pertaining to mobile technology. Steven is also the Chief News and Review Editor for BostonPocketPC.com and has written several detailed reviews and articles on various facets of mobile technology as well. Steven is a Moderator in the Microsoft Answers forums and also co-manages the New England Windows Phone User Group. Steven is employed as a Biomedical Engineer for the VA New England Healthcare System. When he has some free time he generally spends it with his family or outdoors playing soccer, hitting the slopes, strumming his guitar, catching a movie in his self-constructed custom home theater, or riding the trails on his mountain bike.

Acknowledgments

Putting together a book such as this is a group effort, and I'd like to take a few moments to thank a few key people.

First, I'd like to thank the team at Apress for their help and guidance, especially Mark Beckner, Kelly Moritz, Laurin Becker, Pat Meador, and Jim Markham. Their helpful suggestions and support have turned pages on my computer screen into the book you're holding now.

A second group that I must thank for their help in compiling this book include my friends at Microsoft, specifically Mike Fosmire, PJ Forgione, Beth Goza, and Andrew Brown. I also need to recognize the help, support, and suggestions I've received from fellow Microsoft MVPs, specifically Jason Dunn, Don Sorcinelli, Steven Hughes, Johan van Mierlo, Jack Cook, Chris Leckness, Eric Hicks, Ed Hansberry, Darius Wey, Todd Ogasawara, Adam Lein, Dave Matson, and Nuno Luz. I also can't forget others in the "blogosphere" that have helped me as I've written over the years, include Janak Parekh, Judie Lipsett Stanford, Vincent Ferrari, Doug Raeburn, Ashley Dunn, and Jason Lee.

Finally I would like to recognize the contributions of my family and friends, especially my wife, Karey, as she provided much needed assistance in preparing the over 400 images that this book uses. Think of her whenever you see a "Tap" finger! I'm also indebted to my parents, Alan and Dianne, who indulged my love of technology from an early age so that I could go forth and do things like earn PhDs, write books, and be successful. I also very much appreciate the support and encouragement of Karey's family (Dan, Sue, Greg, Scott, & Mark, as well as numerous aunts, uncles, and cousins!) over the past 11 years. I also cannot forget my friends, coworkers, and mentors who also played a significant role in both supporting me and building me into the type of person who is disciplined enough to write books under tight deadlines. These people include Irma & Mike Babij, Dave, Linda, Jim, and Katie Spurrier, Steve Jocke, Tony Rylow, Ashley Newman, Maria Gaglio, Erika Rylow, Trella Williams, Marie Batteiger, Michael Batteiger, Matt Rozema, Holly Feiler, Maggie Herceg, Christina McKenzie, Paul Culbertson, Tara Reineck, Pat Hinkle, Cindy Kriska, and others from my high school and college days. Also included are my mentors, Drs. JD Jasper, Eric Johnson, Elke Weber, Stephen Christman, Rickye Heffner, Harvard Armus, and my co-workers, Martine Baldassi, Bernd Figner, Ye Li, Eric Schoenberg, Annie Ma, Hiro Kotabe, Seoungwoo Lee, Shu Sun, Myoungsun Namkung, Marie Chesaniuk, Cindy Kim, Margaret Lee, Kirstin Appelt, David Hardisty, Maria Hamilton, Julie Smith, Ray Crookes, Lisa Zaval, Katherine Thompson, and Galen Treur.

Part I

Quick Start Guide

In your hands is one of a select group of smartphones, Windows Phone 7 from Microsoft. This Quick Start Guide will help get you and your new Windows phone up and running by pointing out common tasks you might want to do (such as set up your email or contacts) and giving you a quick introduction to these features. After each quick feature introduction, I'll point you to where in third part of the book you can find more information on each item. In no time, you'll be up-to-speed and ready-to-go with your new Windows Phone 7!

The Windows Phone 7 Interface

While Windows Phone 7 shares the "Windows" name with other Microsoft products, it does not share the same interface. For example, it does not feature the familiar **Start** menu or a mouse-centric approach. Instead, the Windows Phone 7 interface has been designed from the ground up to be easy to use, quick, and responsive. This section shows off the interface and talks about how to navigate through the parts of your phone that you will be using frequently.

Turning on your Windows Phone 7 device shows a **Lock** screen with the date, time, and other information. Use your finger to slide the screen up and reveal the **Start** screen.

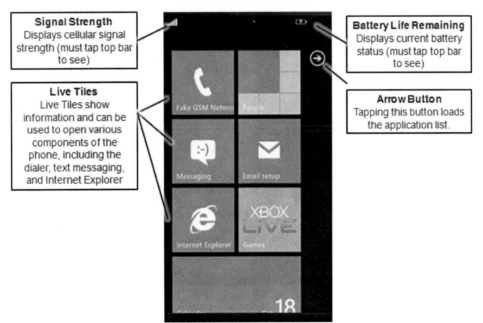

Signal Strength
Displays cellular signal strength (must tap top bar to see)

Battery Life Remaining
Displays current battery status (must tap top bar to see)

Live Tiles
Live Tiles show information and can be used to open various components of the phone, including the dialer, text messaging, and Internet Explorer

Arrow Button
Tapping this button loads the application list.

NOTE: All Windows Phone 7 devices have a Windows, Search, and Back button on the front of the phone, along with a power button and camera button on the sides. The exact placement, however, is up to the phone manufacturer. To locate these buttons on your specific Windows Phone 7 device, consult your user's manual.

The **Start** screen consists of a variety of *live tiles*. Each live tile shows information regarding that application on the phone. For example, the **Calendar** live tile shows your next appointment. The **Messaging** and Inbox tiles show how many unread messages you have. You can have a virtually unlimited amount of tiles that you can customize by putting them in whatever order or location you'd like. Pressing and holding any tile for a few seconds will highlight it, allowing you to move it around.

Programs that do not have a tile on the **Start** screen can be accessed by pressing the **Arrow** icon in the upper-right corner. Pressing the **Arrow** icon will show the **applications list**. This list shows all of the applications installed on your phone, allowing you to access any of them. You can also press and hold any icon to bring up a menu that will allow you to pin the app to the **Start** screen.

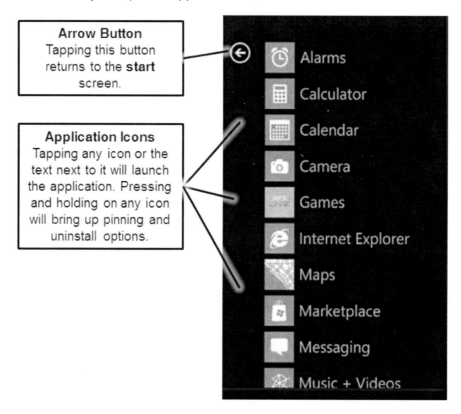

Arrow Button
Tapping this button returns to the **start** screen.

Application Icons
Tapping any icon or the text next to it will launch the application. Pressing and holding on any icon will bring up pinning and uninstall options.

Alarms
Calculator
Calendar
Camera
Games
Internet Explorer
Maps
Marketplace
Messaging
Music + Videos

You will see a variety of types of screens in the applications you use on your phone. For example, the following screen displays a **Pivot** view, which is used by many applications to show your configuration options. **Pivot** views consist of lists with a number of options that are grouped under headings. You can access the following **Pivot** view by pressing the **Settings** icon on the **applications list**.

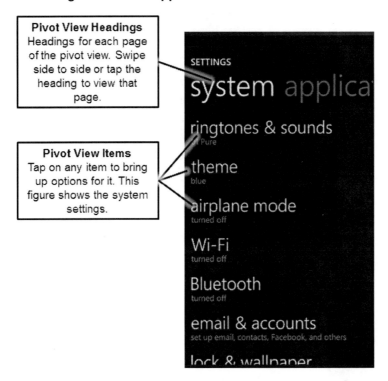

Pivot View Headings
Headings for each page of the pivot view. Swipe side to side or tap the heading to view that page.

Pivot View Items
Tap on any item to bring up options for it. This figure shows the system settings.

Within any screen, you may also come across listboxes and checkboxes, as shown in the preceding screenshot. These options behave similarly to how they behave on your computer – however, instead of dropping down a list of options, the listbox (when clicked) displays a list of options to choose from. Checkboxes toggle on or off the setting described in the text next to them.

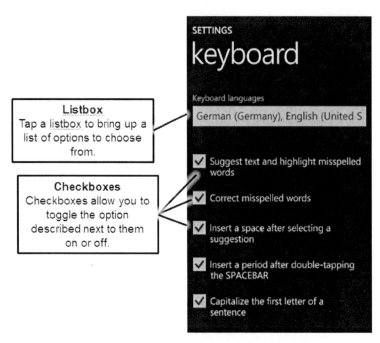

Another control frequently found in Windows Phone 7 is the slider. A slider control lets you toggle an option on or off. In the example that follows, the Wi-Fi radio has been toggled to **On**. Pressing the slider again would set the Wi-Fi radio to **Off**.

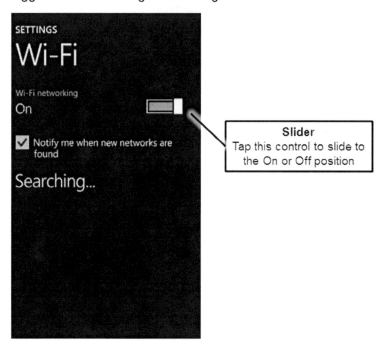

Finally, another type of screen you're likely to encounter in Windows Phone 7 is a **Panorama** view. Like a **Pivot** view, a *Panorama view* shows a number of items with a movable background. The example that follows shows the **Pictures** Hub. The outline of the device represents one page that would be shown in the **Panorama** view; the user can swipe her finger from side-to-side to bring up the previous or next page.

Using a Windows Phone 7 device is pretty simple. Table QS-1 lists a few finger gestures you will find helpful as you navigate your device's screens.

Table QS-1. *Finger Gestures*

Gesture Name	Looks Like	Does
Tap		Opens an item you tap once.
Double Tap		Zooms in or out on various views, such as pictures, web pages, and maps.
Tap and Hold		Opens menus specific to that item (e.g., the menu to pin an item to the **Start** screen)
Pan		Moves through screens in the **Panorama** or **Pivot** views.
Flick		Moves rapidly through a series of items.

Gesture Name	Looks Like	Does
Pinch and Stretch		Zooms in or out with more precision than double tapping, allowing you to control how far in or out you zoom.

With the gestures and the interface descriptions listed in Table QS-1, you're now ready to start using your phone. The "Condensed Steps" section that follows will get you up-and-running with common tasks – or you can head over to the chapters in Part 3 to start learning about your device in depth!

Condensed Steps

The bulk of this book (Part 3) contains chapters on pretty much anything you'd want to do with your Windows Phone 7 device. As a new Windows Phone user, however, you might have a very specific query (e.g., "How do I set up my Bluetooth headset?") that you simply want me to answer by pointing you in the right direction. This section will do precisely that, using a question-and-answer format. It lists common questions and provides short answers; it also indicates where in Part 3 you can get more information if you need it.

Basic Phone Functions

Table QS-2 lists basic phone functions and where you can find out more about each function.

Table QS-2. *Basic Phone Functions. (Note that all the steps that follow assume you have turned on and unlocked your phone, and that you are at the Start screen.)*

Question	Answer		Where to Learn More
How do I make a phone call?		Tap the **Phone** live tile.	Chapter 2: "Making Phone Calls"
		Press the **Dialpad** button and dial the number.	
		Finally, press **call**.	
How do I send a text message?		Tap the **Messaging** live tile.	Chapter 13: "Using Text Messages".
		Press the **New** button. Enter the name or number of the person you want to text and the message.	
		Finally, press **send**.	
How do I change the background from black to white?		Press the **Arrow** button in the upper right to access the **applications list**. Then, at the bottom, choose **Settings**. Tap **theme** and change **Background** from **dark** to **light**.	Chapter 6: "Customizing Your Phone".

Question	Answer		Where to Learn More
How do I look up someone's contact information?	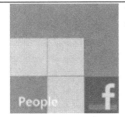	Tap the **People** live tile, then tap a person's name to view his contact information.	Chapter 10: "Connecting With People: Using the People Live Tile"
How do I set up my email account?		Tap the **Email Setup** button and choose the type of email account you would like to set up. Finally, follow the prompts to enter your information.	Chapter 3: "Setting up Accounts"
How do I see my next appointment?			Chapter 12: "Using and Customizing the Calendar"

Simply view the **Calendar** live tile; it will show your next appointment at the top.

Smartphone Functions

Table QS-3 lists features and functions that you'd expect a smartphone to be capable of; it also explains how to accomplish these tasks on your Windows Phone 7 device.

Table QS-3. *Smartphone Functions. (Note that all the steps that follow assume you have turned on and unlocked your phone, and that you are at the* **Start** *screen.)*

Question	Answer		Where to Learn More
How do I open a web page?		Tap the **Internet Explorer** live tile.	Chapter 14: "Surfing the Web Using Internet Explorer"
	http://www.microsoft.com/windowsphone	Tap the address bar.	
		Finally, use the keyboard to type in the address of the page you would like to view, and hit the **Right arrow** key.	
How do I bookmark a web page?		Tap the **Add** button while viewing any web page.	Chapter 14: "Surfing the Web Using Internet Explorer"
What is the quickest way to take a picture?	Press and hold the **Camera** button for approximately three seconds. The **Camera** app will open. Press the **Camera** button again to take a picture.		Chapter 15: "Taking Pictures and Putting Them Online"
How do I put my music (from my computer) onto my phone?	Use the **Zune** desktop software to accomplish this. Once **Zune** is installed, use the micro-USB cable included with your Windows Phone 7 device to connect it to your computer. Follow the prompts to set up the software.		Chapter 23: "Connecting to the Zune Software"

Question	Answer		Where to Learn More
How do I find new applications and games?		Finally, tap the **Marketplace** live tile and explore (or search) for products you might like. You can install them directly from your phone.	Chapter 25: "Exploring the Marketplace"
Is there a calculator?	Yes. Tap the **Arrow** icon at the upper right of the **Start** screen, and then tap the **Calculator** icon.		(The calculator is pretty self-explanatory!)

Microsoft Exclusives

Table QS-4 lists things exclusive to your Windows Phone 7 smartphone and explains how to start exploring them.

Table QS-4. *Microsoft Exclusives. (Note that all the steps that follow assume you have turned on and unlocked your phone, and that you are at the **Start** screen.)*

Question	Answer		Where to Learn More
How do I open a **Word**, **Excel**, or **PowerPoint** document?	The easiest way to open an **Office** file is to email it to yourself and then tap the file from within the email. If the file is already on your device, you can use the **Office Hub** to open it.		Chapters 18-20
How do I enter a note in **OneNote**?		Tap the **Arrow** icon in the upper right to access the **applications list**.	Chapter 17: "Using Microsoft Office OneNote Mobile"
		Tap the **Office** icon.	
		Finally, tap **new note** to enter a new note.	

Question	Answer		Where to Learn More
How do I manage my Xbox LIVE avatar?		Tap the **Xbox LIVE Games** live tile. If you are signed in with your Windows Live ID, you will see your avatar. Tap your avatar to modify it.	Chapter 24: "Using Your Phone With Xbox LIVE"
How can I quickly see what my friends are up to?		Tap the **People** live tile and slide the screen to the right to show the **what's new** section.	Chapter 10: "Connecting With People: Using the People Live Tile"
How do I get Bing Maps to show me where someone's address is?	See the preceding entry on how to look up a person's contact information. Once you have that up, tap the **map work address** button. map work address		Chapter 10: "Connecting With People: Using the People Live Tile"
How do I access my company's **SharePoint** server?	Depending on the type of **SharePoint** server your company is running, you may be able to access it through the **Office Hub**. Office Or, you might have to use **Internet Explorer** (see Chapter 21 for more information).		Chapter 21: "Connecting to SharePoint"

Settings and Configuration

Table QS-5 discusses the various settings and configuration items you may want to work with, including how to connect to different networks and use a Bluetooth device.

Table QS-5. *Settings and Configuration. (Note that all the steps that follow assume you have turned on and unlocked your phone, and that you are at the **Start** screen.)*

Question	Answer	Where to Learn More
How do I set up a Bluetooth headset?	Press the **Arrow** button in the upper right to access the **applications list**. Then at the bottom, choose **Settings**. In settings tap on *Bluetooth* Turn Bluetooth on. Make sure your headset is in **Discoverable** mode; it should appear under the list of discovered devices. Tap your headset to start the pairing process.	Chapter 7: "Setting up Bluetooth and Wi-Fi"
How do I connect to a Wi-Fi network?	Press the **Arrow** button in the upper right to access the **applications list**. At the bottom, choose **Settings**, and then tap **Wi-Fi**. Turn Wi-Fi on. Your Wi-Fi network should appear in the list of discovered networks. Tap your network and enter any security key required to connect. Your phone will now automatically connect to this network in the future.	Chapter 7: "Setting up Bluetooth and Wi-Fi"
How do I change my ringtone?	Press the **arrow** button in the upper right to access the **applications list**. Then at the bottom, choose **Settings**. In settings tap on *ringtones & sounds*.	Chapter 6: "Customizing Your Phone"

Question		Answer	Where to Learn More
How do I set a PIN code required to unlock my phone?		Press the **arrow** button in the upper right to access the **applications list**. Then at the bottom, choose **Settings**. In settings tap on *lock and wallpaper*. Then tap on the *password* slider to change it to "on", and enter your desired PIN code.	Chapter 8: "Managing and Securing Your Phone"
How do I change keyboard settings?		Press the **arrow** button in the upper right to access the **applications list**. Then at the bottom, choose **Settings**. In settings tap on *keyboard* to adjust options related to spell checking, spacing, and capitalization.	Chapter 6: "Customizing Your Phone"
How do I adjust the screen brightness?		Press the **arrow** button in the upper right to access the **applications list**. Then at the bottom, choose **Settings**. In settings tap on *brightness* to modify the settings.	Chapter 6: "Customizing Your Phone"

Part II

Introduction

Welcome to your new Windows Phone 7—and to the book that tells you what you need to know to get the most out of it! In this part, I show you how the book is organized and where to go to find what you need. From there, you can jump right in and be on your way to Windows Phone 7 productivity and happiness!

Welcome to Windows Phone 7!

Has anyone ever complimented you on your excellent taste in mobile phones? If not, let me be the first—you've made a great decision by choosing a Windows Phone 7 smartphone. Microsoft has put a lot of hard work into Windows Phone 7, starting pretty much from scratch and creating a brand new operating system, the goal of which is to make your life easier by freeing you from staring at your phone!

How does this work? How can a phone save you from other phones? Simply by showing you what you need to know in a quick and concise fashion, allowing you to glance at your phone rather than study the screen intently while life passes you by. For example, your **Start** screen on a Windows Phone 7 device includes live tiles, not icons. What is the difference? Well, a *live tile* changes—it shows you your next appointment on the **Calendar** tile, it shows you recent status updates from friends if you create a tile for them, and it shows you at a quick glance how many messages or emails you have waiting for you.

Windows Phone 7 also integrates everything into it that you'd expect in a modern smartphone. The five megapixel camera can grab life's moments quickly and post those photos straight to Facebook. The built-in radio and large storage capacity keep you entertained with music, videos, and more. And the Marketplace, which features the Zune music store, has a plethora of things to explore. We'll talk about all of these features throughout this book!

Getting the Most out of Windows Phone 7 Made Simple

One way to approach this book is to read it from cover-to-cover, and learn everything about your Windows Phone 7 in a logical progression. I start the book by discussing the initial setup of your phone, including how to configure it the first time you power it on, how to make phone calls, how to add email accounts, and how to customize the screen the way you like. I then move into other activities that are a little less crucial, such as text messaging, alarms, the calendar, and contacts. Next, I discuss the most powerful (and perhaps most fun) things you can accomplish toward the end—the built in **Microsoft Office** applications, the integration with **Zune** software on your PC, and the ability to use your phone with Xbox LIVE. Finally, I explain how to update your phone and where to find some additional resources.

However, if you're not really looking for a beginning-to-end read, you can also jump right into any chapter that interests you. If I mention something I've covered before (or will cover in future chapters), I point you to where you can find more information about that topic. And throughout all of the material, I try not to use any confusing "tech jargon"; what I'm saying not only gets the job done, it also makes sense!

Windows Phone 7, the Name

This book is meant for all users of a Windows Phone 7 smartphone. Since Microsoft believes that a variety of companies are capable of producing quality Windows Phone 7 phones, I don't target one specific device—all the available phones should provide the same experience. At the time of writing, T-Mobile and AT&T (in the United States) both have multiple Windows Phone 7 devices, all of which can be used with the steps and material discussed in this book.

Navigating This Book

This book consists of three parts: "Part I: Quick Start Guide"; "Part II: Introduction"; and "Part III: Your Windows Phone 7." Here I provide an overview of what you find in these parts.

Day in the Life of a Windows Phone 7 User

Located inside the front and back covers, the "Day in the Life of a Windows Phone 7 User" reference provides a realistic look at my typical day using a Windows Phone 7 device. Along the way, I point out where in this book you can find out more information on these topics as I engage in such exciting tasks as reviewing a **PowerPoint** presentation or taking a picture.

Part I: Quick Start Guide

The Quick Start Guide covers two important subjects:

- **The Windows Phone 7 Interface**: Learn about the various tiles, buttons, and types of screens you'll see on your Windows Phone 7 device!

■ **Condensed Steps:** The instructions in this book are generally very specific and leave no details to chance. However, if you simply want to know where something is so you can "wing it" and set it up on your own, I'll provide the virtual roadmap to let you do so. I'll also let you know where you can find more information.

Part II: Introduction

You're reading it.

Part III: Your Windows Phone 7

These are the 27 chapters I alluded to earlier. These chapters start with your Windows Phone 7 device's most basic phone functions, then gradually shift gears to tackle its most powerful features. These chapters cover the topics in depth, teaching you how to accomplish common tasks on your Windows Phone 7 device through a series of practical, how-to steps!

Quickly Locating Tips and Notes

If you flip through this book, you can instantly see specially formatted **TIPS** and **NOTES** that discuss important things to consider when using your phone to accomplish various tasks.

> **TIPS** and **NOTES** are formatted like this, with a gray background, to help you see them more quickly.

Feedback!

Whenever I do any form of teaching, whether in a classroom or in a book or on a blog, I encourage people to give me feedback and ask questions. Reading this book certainly classifies you as a virtual student and, as such, my virtual "door" is always open. You can get in touch with me through my blog at `www.jonwestfall.com` or through Twitter (@jonwestfall).

Part **III**

You and Your Windows Phone 7...

This is the heart of *Windows Phone 7 Made Simple*. Here, you'll find clearly labeled chapters –each explaining features of your Windows Phone 7 device. You'll see that most chapters focus on an individual part of the phone or a specific type of application. Most of the chapters discuss applications that come with your Windows Phone 7 device, but I've also included a chapter devoted to the ever-growing Windows Phone Marketplace. Finally, the last two chapters are devoted to updating your phone (when updates become available) and additional resources you can explore, respectively.

Chapter 1

Setting up Your Windows Phone

Welcome! And congratulations on buying a phone that, as the marketing material suggests, might just free you from staring at your phone all the time! This book will take you step-by-step through the process of configuring and setting up your new phone. We'll start with what you'll see as soon as you power up your phone for the first time, and then go on to talk about what makes your Windows Phone 7 device unique. Along the way, I'll be sure to give you the best tips and tricks I've discovered while using Windows Phone 7.

What Is Windows Phone 7?

Windows Phone 7 is the latest operating system for mobile phones by Microsoft, the publisher of Windows on desktop computers. Previously, Microsoft created and sold software called "Windows Mobile," which ran on smartphones and looked very similar to how Windows appears on desktop computers, **Start** menu and all. However, all of that has now changed!

I first learned about Windows Phone 7 (then called Windows Mobile 7) a few years ago. At the time, in super-secret sessions about which I am legally not allowed to speak (and really don't want to anyway), it appeared to be an interesting product, but nothing too revolutionary or new. However, as Microsoft watched the world change with regard to how people use smartphones, it came to realize that it needed to change course and produce an excellent mobile experience. Windows Phone 7, in its current form, was born. The device you're holding (or possibly have lying next to this book) is one of many Windows Phone 7 devices made by a variety of manufacturers. While they're all physically different (e.g., in terms of style, shape, and color), they all run the same software: Windows Phone 7. That's why this book isn't written toward a specific device—it doesn't have to be. All Windows Phone 7 devices share many common characteristics, including the following:

Three buttons on the front of the device called **Start**, **back**, and **search**—These buttons are pretty self-explanatory. The **Start** button takes you to your **Start** screen, which we'll discuss in this chapter. The **back** button takes you back to whatever you were working on previously. The **search** button behaves a bit differently, depending on what you're doing. Most of the time, clicking this button brings up Bing search, enabling you to search for things on the Web, in the news, and in your area.

A dedicated **Camera** button and (at least) a five megapixel camera—This camera lets your phone take quality photos wherever you go and upload them automatically if you choose to post them to the Web.

A built-in GPS and accelerometer—These features let you navigate to wherever you wish to go, see a map of your current location, or rotate your phone to view things in **Portrait** or **Landscape** mode.

Four-point multitouch screen—Your device's screen allows you to use up to four fingers on the screen at once, if you're flexible enough. The screen also features a WVGA resolution (800x480).

A 1 GHz ARM v7 or better processor—This processor includes at least 256 MB of RAM and 8 GB of memory, as well as a DirectX 9-capable GPU so that graphics can be rendered properly.

In a break from previous versions of Windows Mobile, developers now know that the preceding list of features (and several others) will definitely be included on a Windows Phone 7 device. This means developers can build software that takes advantage of any of these features, and all Windows Phone 7 users will able to benefit from their efforts.

Before we get started, we need to get your phone set up and ready to go. Follow the steps listed in the following sections to embark on your Windows Phone 7 journey!

Powering Up

The first step in using your phone is to turn it on for the first time. Make sure that your phone has a fully charged battery inserted or simply keep the phone plugged in as you go through the initial setup process; this will ensure that it has enough power to complete the setup process. Also be sure to check that your SIM card is in place if you use a network that relies on SIM cards, such as AT&T or T-Mobile in the United States. Follow these steps to set up your Windows Phone 7 device:

1. Press the **Power** button to turn on your phone. You should see a series of screens that identify the manufacturer of the phone and a **Windows Phone** splash screen. Once you get to the screen that says **Welcome to your phone**, you're ready to go. The screen should look similar to the one shown in Figure 1–1.

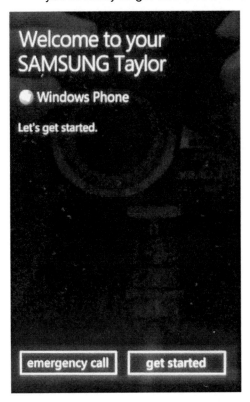

Figure 1–1. *Getting started on your Windows Phone 7 device.*

2. From this screen, you can either begin the setup process (click the **get started** button) or dial an emergency number in case you power on your phone for the first time and a crisis erupts (click the **emergency call** button). Clicking the **emergency call** button will bring up a screen similar to the one shown in Figure 1–2. The **Emergency calls only** screen enables you to dial an emergency service if needed (e.g., 911).

Figure 1–2. *Placing an emergency call.*

3. Assuming no emergencies are taking place while setting up your phone, tap **get started** to begin setting up your phone.

4. The **Choose a Language** screen lets you choose the language you'd like your phone to use (see Figure 1–3). This book will show screens using the **English (United States)** setting; however, you can use whichever language setting you prefer. Simply tap the language of your choice and then press **next**.

Figure 1–3._Choosing a language._

5. The next screen lets you view the **Windows Phone Terms of Use** and the **Privacy Statement** (see Figure 1–4). You must accept the terms outlined to use your phone to do anything other than make an emergency call. If you hit **reject**, you'll get a message that explains this. Assuming you don't find anything objectionable in these documents, press **accept** to move on.

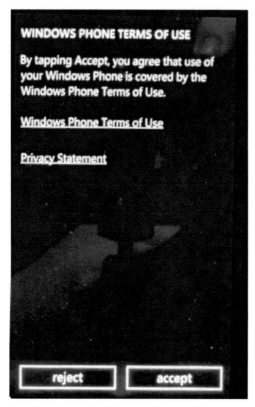

Figure 1–4. *The Windows Phone Terms of Use.*

6. On the **Windows Phone Settings** screen, you'll be asked how you want your Windows Phone configured (see Figure 1–5). You can accept the default settings by pressing **recommended** or modify your phone's settings by pressing **custom**. Pressing **custom** will bring up the **Custom Windows Phone Settings** screen, which will look similar to the screen shown in Figure 1–6. This screen lets you turn on or off cellular data usage (which you will likely want to keep enabled, unless you do not have a cellular data plan). You can also elect to send information to Microsoft that will help it improve future Windows Phone devices. This information is anonymous; it merely lets Microsoft know how you're using your phone, so that it can continue to build great phones. Once you're done with this screen, press **next**.

Figure 1–5. *Choosing between recommended and custom settings.*

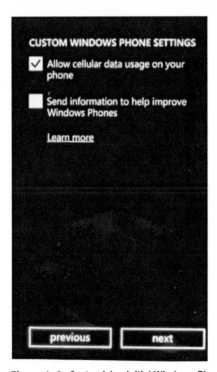

Figure 1–6. *Customizing initial Windows Phone settings.*

7. The **Choose Time Zone** screen allows you to choose your time zone (see Figure 1–7). Choose the appropriate time zone and press **next**.

Figure 1–7. *Choosing your time zone.*

8. You'll then be taken to the **Sign In With a Windows Live ID** screen (see Figure 1–8). Signing in with a Windows Live ID allows you to synchronize your Windows Live information (e.g., your Zune Pass, Xbox Live, Hotmail, and Messenger data) to your phone. You can either **sign in** with an existing Live ID; **create one** that you'll use on your phone, online, and on an Xbox; or choose **not now** and set one up later. You do not need to set one up now; so, if you would like to wait, go ahead and do so. You can always set this account up later!

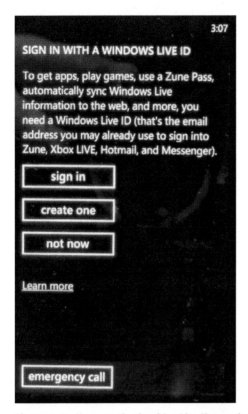

Figure 1–8. *You may sign in with a Live ID or wait until later.*

NOTE: The first Windows Live ID you sign in with on your phone is special—it's the one that will be tied to both Zune and Xbox Live. If you have multiple Windows Live IDs or Hotmail accounts, be sure to sign into the one you use for Zune and Xbox first (if you use these services already). You can add other accounts later and have the email from these accounts synchronize to your device without issue.

9. Once you've finished with the Windows Live step, you should see an **All Done** screen (see Figure 1–9). Press **done** and the initial setup process is complete!

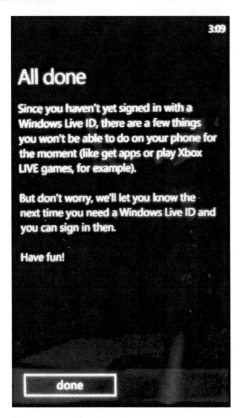

Figure 1–9. *Setup complete.*

10. You'll be taken to your **Start** screen, which initially is pretty plain. However, this screen can easily be modified to your liking. In the rest of this chapter, we'll discuss some common things that apply to many parts of your Windows Phone, such as the **Start** screen, the **applications list**, and the **settings** app. We'll also discuss what a live tile is, since those squares on your **Start** screen are much more interesting that just a plain old icon or picture!

> **NOTE:** When you turn on your phone's screen after following the preceding steps, you'll see a full-screen picture with the date, time, and your next appointment on it. This is called the **Lock** screen, and it is meant to keep you from accidentally doing things with your phone while it's in your bag or pocket. To get back to your **Start** screen, simply slide your finger upward on the screen to "roll away" the **Lock** screen image. If you have a security code set (see Chapter 8: "Managing and Securing Your Phone"), you'll need to enter that code to get back to your **Start** screen.

Your Start Screen and Live Tiles

You'll notice that your **Start** screen is filled with many large squares (and a few rectangles). Each of these tiles is referred to as a *live tile*, and each does something different when you tap it. Most of this book is dedicated to specific live tiles and how you use them. We'll discuss each of the default tiles (see Figure 1–10) in Table 1–1.

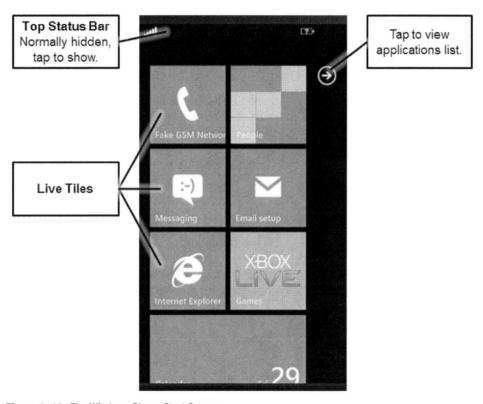

Figure 1–10. *The Windows Phone Start Screen.*

Table 1-1. *Default Windows Phone start screen live tiles.*

Tile	What It Does
	The **Phone** live tile provides your device's most basic functionality: it lets you make a basic phone call. In addition to a number pad, it also houses your call log and includes buttons to access your voicemail and the **People** live tile. A number on this tile tells you that you have missed calls.
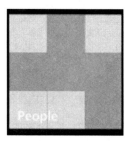	The **People** live tile normally shows pictures of your friends and contacts in the smaller squares within it. Tapping it will bring up a list of all of your contacts, as well as recent status updates by them!
	The **Messaging** live tile lets you send and receive text messages. These messages can include both text and pictures! A number on this tile tells you how many unread text messages you have.
	This **Email setup** tile only appears until you set up your first account. Afterward, this becomes the tile for that account. A number on this tile shows how many unread emails you have. Note that you can have multiple email tiles—one for each account!
	The **Internet Explorer** live tile lets you launch the built-in web browser. From this program, you can view web pages just as you would on your computer. Note that many of these pages will be specially formatted for the smaller size of your phone's screen!

Tile	What It Does
	The **XBOX Live** live tile lets you browse through Xbox games you've installed, customize your avatar, and challenge others to games!
	The **Calendar** live tile shows your next appointment. Tapping this tile will bring up your full **Calendar** view.
	The **Pictures** live tile lets you access pictures you've taken with your device's camera, pictures you've stored on Facebook and Windows Live SkyDrive, and pictures others have uploaded to these services! You can change the picture that serves as the background of this tile—we'll discuss how in several of this book's chapters.
	The **Music and Videos** live tile lets you access the music you've stored on your device or stream music using the Zune media player and your Zune Pass. You can also watch videos and access your device's built in FM radio.

Tile	What It Does
	The **Marketplace** live tile launches the Windows Phone **Marketplace** app, which lets you browse and download new applications, music, videos, and more!

As you can see, your Windows Phone includes a wide variety of useful and interesting features. You can use this book in one of two ways. First, you can read it straight through, starting here and continuing to the end. In the process of doing so, you'll learn about everything your Windows Phone 7 device can do in easy-to-understand language and with many step-by-step examples. Second, you can use this book as a reference, flipping to sections you want to know more about as you explore your Windows Phone 7 device. Whichever approach you choose, I hope you'll have fun finding out how to use your Windows Phone 7 device to its full potential!

Chapter 2

Making Phone Calls

Even with a fancy smartphone like your Windows Phone 7 device, sometimes all one needs or wants from a phone is the ability to make a call. This chapter will show you all the different ways you can place a call from your Windows Phone 7 smartphone, including a few smart ways to get connected fast!

Dialing a Number

Know the number of your favorite pizza place by heart (while ironically not knowing your spouse's)? Dialing a number is a pretty simple affair.

1. Turn on your phone and unlock it. Then press the **Phone** live tile. It should be displaying the current cellular network you're connected to (i.e., "AT&T" or "T-Mobile").

2. A screen similar to that shown in Figure 2–1 will appear, showing by default your call history, or recently called numbers.

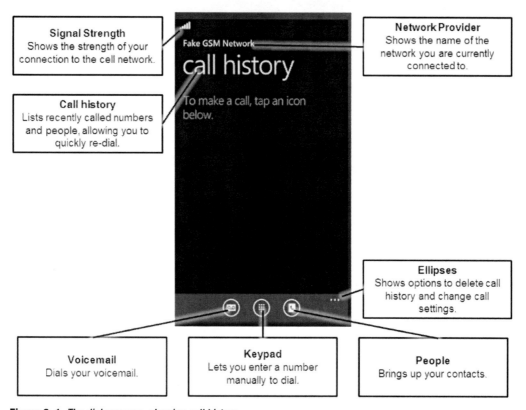

Signal Strength
Shows the strength of your connection to the cell network.

Network Provider
Shows the name of the network you are currently connected to.

Call history
Lists recently called numbers and people, allowing you to quickly re-dial.

call history

To make a call, tap an icon below.

Fake GSM Network

Ellipses
Shows options to delete call history and change call settings.

Voicemail
Dials your voicemail.

Keypad
Lets you enter a number manually to dial.

People
Brings up your contacts.

Figure 2–1. *The dialer screen, showing call history.*

3. Tap the **Keypad** button at the bottom of the screen to bring up the numeric keypad.

4. Dial the number you wish to call and press **call**. If you wish to simply save the number to one of your contacts, you can press the **save** button. This will launch the contact picker, allowing you to attach it to an existing contact or create a new one—perfect for those times when someone gives you their number and you need to jot it down quickly!

5. While on the call, the screen shows an **end call** button [end call], a **keypad** button that you'll use if you need to enter numbers while on the call (for example, navigating a customer service phone system), and a button with two small arrows that show more options. Tap that button (see Figure 2–2) to access in-call options.

Figure 2–2. *Call options.*

6. The in-call options let you choose to activate the **Speaker** phone, **Mute** your side of the call so that the other party can't hear you sneeze, **hold** the call, and **add calls** to the current call—or create a conference call.

7. When you're done with your call, click **end call** and the call will be terminated. You'll see that the number you dialed (or name of the person) now appears in the call history.

TIP: If you want to delete your call history, you can do so by pressing the **Ellipsis** button ••• (Figure 2–1) and choosing "delete all" from the options that appear.

Dialing a Person from Your Contacts

Windows Phone 7 allows you to call people from your contacts through a few different ways. The following steps assume you're already in the phone dialer (showing the "call history" screen as shown in Figure 2–1). However, you could also start from the **Start** screen and press the **People** live tile. We'll discuss more about this tile in a later chapter.

1. From the phone screen (Figure 2–1), press the **People** button. A list of your contacts should appear.

2. Tap the name of the person you'd like to call (see Figure 2–3).

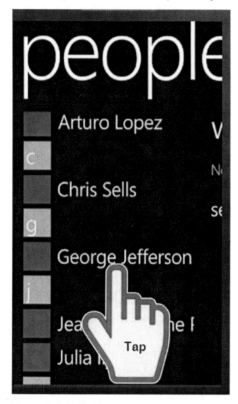

Figure 2–3. *Selecting a contact.*

3. A screen will appear listing the information you have stored about that person. From here you can tap on the text link to "call mobile" or "call home" (see Figure 2–4).

Figure 2–4. *Tapping the mobile number to make a call.*

4. Tapping the text will cause the phone to dial, and you'll see a screen similar to Figure 2–2, with the same options available to put the call on speaker phone, mute, end, etc.

Configuring Call Settings

Windows Phone 7 offers a number of settings (described below) that let you modify how calls are made or received, as well as setting a PIN code required to make a call ("SIM PIN"). To access call settings, from the phone screen (Figure 2–1), press the **Ellipsis** button and choose "call settings." A screen similar to Figure 2–5 will appear.

Figure 2–5. *Phone settings.*

- **My phone number**: The first entry on the page displays your phone number—the phone number assigned to the SIM card currently inserted into the device or the phone number programmed into the device by your cellular provider.

- **Voicemail number**: The second number shows your voicemail number. You should not normally have to change this value unless you use a third-party voicemail system other than your cellular provider.

- **Show my caller ID to**: The next setting lets you control who can see your caller ID information when you make a call. The default, "everyone," sends your caller ID information to every caller you dial. You can also tap on the value to change it to "no one" or "my contacts." "No one" tells your phone not to send your caller ID information to any caller you dial. This can be useful if calling someone you do not wish to give your phone number to—they'll see "Unavailable" or "Private" on their screen when your call comes in. "my contacts" is an intermediate option—it sends your caller ID to people you know and have stored in your phone, while not sending it to new numbers you don't have stored in your contact records.

- **Call forwarding:** Call forwarding lets you specify a phone number that all incoming calls to your phone will be redirected to. This setting is stored by your cellular network, so even if you turn off your phone, your calls will still be forwarded until you disable forwarding.

- **International assist:** This setting lets your phone attempt to help you dial international numbers, by ensuring correct formatting so that your call goes through. If you're experiencing issues dialing an international number, you may try switching this off.

- **SIM security**: If your phone has a SIM card, you can use the **SIM security** settings to configure a PIN number that users must enter to make outgoing calls. This can be useful if others use your phone to look up information but you do not want them making calls. To enable SIM security, tap on the option to slide it to the **On** position. A screen will appear asking for your SIM PIN number (usually set at 0000 or the last four digits of your phone number by default). Enter the PIN, and you'll see settings similar to those in Figure 2–6. From these settings, you can change your SIM PIN or disable SIM security by tapping on the slider and entering your PIN.

Figure 2–6. *SIM Lock settings.*

NOTE: Even with SIM security enabled, your phone can still make emergency calls (e.g., 911) without PIN entry.

Windows Phone 7 can dial phone numbers through other applications as well, (i.e., while finding a location in Maps, or through a person's entry in the **People** live tile and we'll discuss those throughout this book. In general, your phone tries to determine wherever it sees a group of numbers if it is a phone number, and if so, links it to the phone dialer allowing you to tap and dial instantly. We'll see examples of this as we continue on!

Chapter 3

Setting up Accounts

Many of us don't have a single email account, while some of us have accounts that do much more than email, such as store our contacts or calendar. We also may have Windows Live or Hotmail accounts that let us log into various Microsoft services, such as Zune, Xbox Live, MSDN, Technet, SkyDrive, or a number of other things. And finally, it seems most of us have Facebook accounts that we use to connect with our friends and family.

Your Windows Phone 7 device allows you to add all of these accounts, so that you can keep connected easily while on the go. This chapter will walk you through setting up a Windows Live account (two of them, actually!), a Microsoft Exchange account (such as one you might have at your workplace), a Google Gmail account, and a Facebook account. Along the way, you'll see how to enter in additional accounts, including a Yahoo! Mail account and a personal account you might have with your Internet service provider (ISP).

Adding Your Windows Live Account(s)

It's easy to get and set up a Windows Live account (or Hotmail account, as it was known previously). Such an account is quite valuable because it lets you sign in to most Microsoft services; therefore, a single account can unlock a variety of neat things your phone can use. If you only have one Windows Live / Hotmail account, then it's easy to complete this series of steps—you can jump right in. However if you have multiple accounts, you should pay particular attention to the next paragraph!

Your Windows Phone 7 device can support multiple Windows Live / Hotmail accounts. However the first one you sign in to, or add, is special. That's because your phone will treat this account as the account you want to use with Zune and Xbox Live. If you've used either of these services before, it's important to sign in with your phone to the same Windows Live ID you've used previously for Zune and Xbox. Otherwise you won't get the same functionality out of the Zune and Xbox areas of your phone. Your phone will warn you about this when you add a Windows Live account; however, if you're unsure what Windows Live account you used for Zune or Xbox previously, you should find this information out before adding any accounts. This will enable you to make sure you add the correct account first. To find out what Windows Live ID your Xbox Gamertag is associated with, fire up your Xbox and sign in. Next, go to **Settings ➤ Account Management ➤ Windows Live ID** to get the account name. To find out what Live ID account your Zune Tag is associated with, open the **Zune** software on your computer and sign in. Next, right-click your profile picture and choose **Switch User**. The email address listed next to your profile picture on the **Sign In** screen is your Windows Live ID!

> **NOTE:** It is possible to change the Windows Live account that's associated with an Xbox Live or Zune tag through the Web; however, you can only do this one time.

Once you know the Windows Live ID you'd like to use, you're ready to add the account to your phone. (Of course, if you already signed into a Windows Live ID during the initial setup process described in Chapter 1, you can skip these steps unless you have additional Windows Live IDs or Hotmail accounts you would like to add!) Follow these steps to add a Windows Live account to your phone:

1. Turn on and unlock your phone.

2. Tap the arrow in the upper right of the screen to bring up the **applications** list. At the bottom of the list, tap **Settings** (see Figure 3–1).

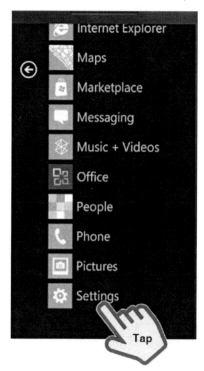

Figure 3–1. *Accessing account settings on your Windows Phone 7.*

3. Tap **email & accounts** (see Figure 3–2).

Figure 3–2. *Accessing **email & accounts**.*

4. Tap **add an account** (see Figure 3–3).

Figure 3–3. *Adding an account.*

5. Tap **Windows Live** to add a Windows Live or Hotmail account (see Figure 3–4).

Figure 3–4. *Adding a Windows Live account.*

6. If this is the first Windows Live account you're adding, you'll see a screen similar to the one shown in Figure 3–5. This screen explains how your first Windows Live ID will be associated with Zune and Xbox. Tap **next** to continue.

Figure 3–5. *Adding your first Windows Live account.*

7.   Enter your Windows Live username (including the part after the @ symbol) and password in the boxes provided (see Figure 3–6), and then press **sign in**. Assuming you entered your information correctly, the account will be added.

Figure 3–6. *Entering your Email address and Password.*

8. If you have more than one Windows Live account to add, press the **start** button on your device and repeat Steps 2 through 7 until you've added all of your desired Windows Live accounts to your phone. Figure 3–7 shows a screen where two accounts have been added to the device.

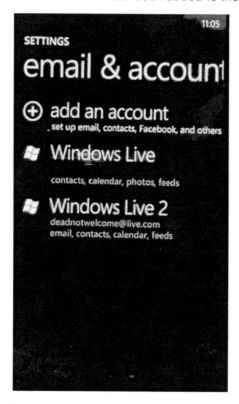

Figure 3–7. *Adding a second Windows Live account.*

9. If you've added an account with a Hotmail or Windows Live mailbox, then you'll see a new **Live Tile** on your **start** screen (see Figure 3–8). Tapping it will let you view the contents of your inbox or send a new message (see Chapter 4: "Using Email" for more information!

Figure 3–8. *Viewing your live tiles.*

Adding Your Work Exchange / Outlook Account

Many of us use **Microsoft Exchange** and **Outlook** at work to connect to and collaborate with others, schedule appointments, and keep track of our contacts. Your phone can access your company's **Exchange** server easily, enabling you to work with email, your calendar, and your contacts with ease. Follow these steps to get started:

1. Turn on and unlock your phone.

2. Tap the arrow in the upper right of the screen to bring up the **applications** list. At the bottom of the list, tap **settings** (see Figure 3–1).

3. Tap **email & accounts** (see Figure 3–2).

4. Tap **add an account** (see Figure 3–3).

5.   Tap **Outlook** (see Figure 3–9).

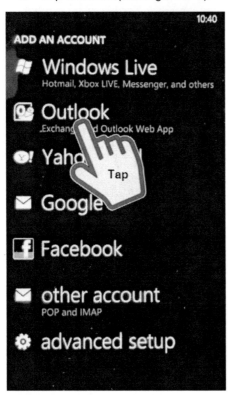

Figure 3–9. *Adding an Outlook account.*

6. Enter your Outlook email address and password in the boxes provided (see Figure 3–10). This is the same username and password you may use to log into your computer at work or to access **Outlook Web Access** when you're not at work. Once you enter this information, press **sign in**.

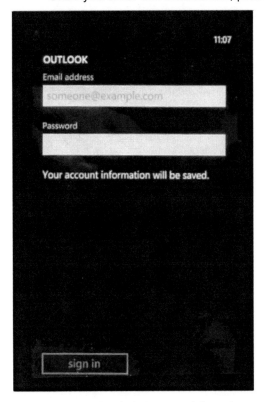

Figure 3–10. *Entering Outlook account information.*

7. You may receive an error asking you to specify your domain name (see Figure 3–11). If you know your domain name, enter it. If not, contact your company's technical support or helpdesk and ask for the necessary information; your company's support or helpdesk should be able to tell you your domain name and any other information your phone may ask for.

Figure 3–11. *Entering your Outlook **Domain** information.*

8. Assuming there are no problems, your account should be added (you'll see it on the **accounts** screen, as shown in Figure 3–12).

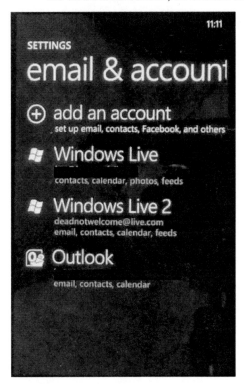

Figure 3–12. *Confirming an added Outlook account.*

9. If you press the **start** button, you should also see a new **Outlook live** tile at the bottom of your **start** screen. You can use this tile to access your **Outlook** inbox from your phone (see Figure 3–13).

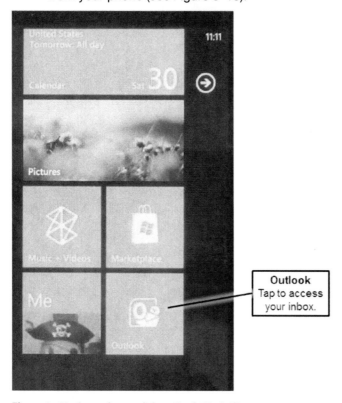

Figure 3–13. *Accessing email from the **Outlook** tile.*

Adding a Google Gmail Account

When not at work, some of us prefer to use Google's Gmail service for our email, calendar, and contacts. Adding it to your phone is very easy. Follow these simple steps to do so:

1. Turn on and unlock your phone.

2. Tap the **Arrow** icon in the upper right of the screen to bring up the **applications** list. At the bottom of the list, tap **settings** (see Figure 3–1).

3. Tap **Email & Accounts** (see Figure 3–2).

4. Tap **add an account** (see Figure 3–3).

5. Tap **Google** (see Figure 3–14).

NOTE: If you use Google Apps for your domain, you can also set this up; however, you may have to do so manually, using the **other account** option shown in Figure 3–14. See Google's **help** section for more information.

Figure 3–14. *Adding a domain for Google Apps.*

6. Enter your Google username and password, and then press **sign in** (see Figure 3–15).

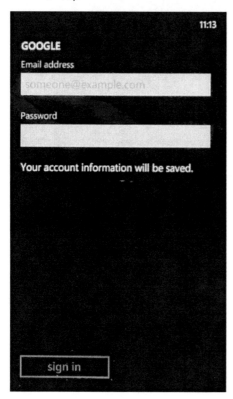

Figure 3–15. *Entering your Google account information.*

7. You should now see **Google** added to your accounts list (see Figure 3–16). If you use **Google Calendar**, you need to complete the following steps to have it synchronize with your phone (if you don't use **Google Calendar**, you can stop now—you're done!).

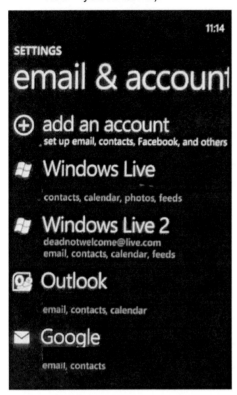

Figure 3–16. *Confirming an added Google account.*

8. To add **Google Calendar**, tap **Google** in the **accounts** list (see Figure 3–16). This brings up the advanced options for **Google Settings**.

9. Tap the box next to **Calendar** to check it (see Figure 3–17), and then press the **Checkmark** button at the bottom to save your changes.

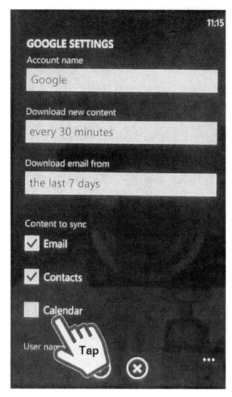

Figure 3–17. *Syncing your Google Calendar.*

10. Your phone should now show the **Google Calendar** app, along with the other calendars you've added!

Adding Other Accounts

To add other accounts, such as a Yahoo! mail account or an account from your Internet service provider (ISP) or job, follow the same steps outlined previously. Obviously, Step 5 will require that you choose the appropriate account, which might include one of the following:

▨   Choose **Yahoo** if you want to add a Yahoo! mail account.

- Choose **Facebook** if you want to enter your Facebook account information. This will provide a rich experience on your phone, enabling you to connect easily with friends; upload photos directly from your phone to Facebook automatically; and view Facebook pictures uploaded by your friends under the **Pictures live** tile. All you need to do to get started is enter your username and password for your Facebook account (see Figure 3–18). Before you know it, you'll have the profile pictures and information for your friends right at your fingertips in the **People live** tile (see Chapter 10:"Connecting with People: Using the People Live Tile") for more information).

Figure 3–18. *Entering Facebook account information.*

- Choose **other account: POP and IMAP** if you would like to add a POP3 or IMAP account provided by your ISP, your domain hosting company, your job, or another service.

- Choose **Advanced Setup** if you have custom values you would like to enter directly. This is typically for more advanced users who may need to specify different ports or protocols to access their mail.

As you can see, adding accounts is easy. In the following chapters we'll discuss how to use the information these accounts have provided to your phone, including how to send and receive e-mail, manage your contacts, and work with your calendar!

Chapter **4**

Using Email

Most of us use email to communicate with our coworkers, family, friends, and just about everyone else these days. Even if you still send letters occasionally, you're probably more likely to drop an email to your coworkers asking about lunch plans than to call them or put a note on their desks. Your Windows Phone 7 device is capable of handling multiple email accounts, letting you read and respond to email, and forwarding messages and composing new ones quickly and easily. We covered adding accounts in the previous chapter; in this chapter, we'll discuss how to work with the inboxes we can now access!

Viewing and Reading Messages

To get started, make sure you've added at least one account (see the previous chapter for more information). Here I'll walk through opening up an inbox and reading a message:

1. Turn on and unlock your phone.

2. Tap an inbox (you choices will likely include **Outlook**, **Hotmail**, **Google Mail**, and/or **Yahoo**, among others, depending on the name of the account).

    You should see a screen similar to Figure 4–1 (it will have your email messages in it, not the more fanciful ones shown in the figure).

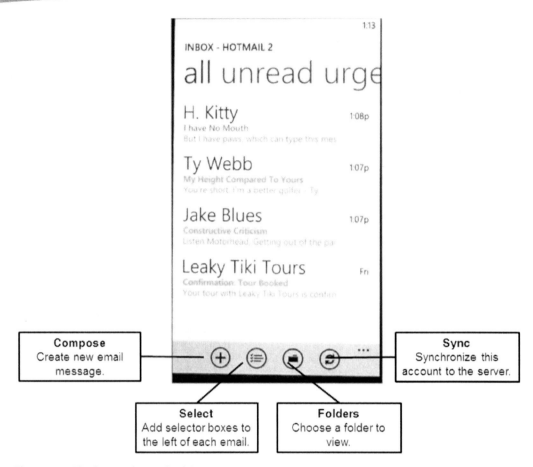

Figure 4–1. *Viewing your interesting inbox.*

3. From this view, you can press and swipe to the left to cycle between all of your messages (as shown in Figure 4–1), unread messages (see Figure 4–2) and urgent messages (see Figure 4–3).

Figure 4–2. *Viewing unread messages.*

Figure 4–3. *Viewing urgent messages.*

4. One of the most frequently performed tasks when managing email is what some refer to as *email triage*, or handling multiple messages at a time. You can select multiple messages by tapping to the left of a sender's name to bring up a series of checkboxes (see Figure 4–4). You can also tap the **select** button (see Figure 4–1) to show the checkboxes.

Figure 4–4. *Managing multiple messages at one time.*

5. After selecting the messages you'd like to work with, you can either click the **delete** button (to delete the messages), the **move** button (to move the messages to a new folder), or tap the **ellipsis (...)** button and choose to mark the messages as read or unread (see Figure 4–5). If you don't want to do anything to the messages, you can simply return to the message list by pressing the **back** button.

Figure 4–5. *Marking messages as read or unread.*

6. Reading a message is very easy; simply tap the message subject to read a given message (see Figure 4–6).

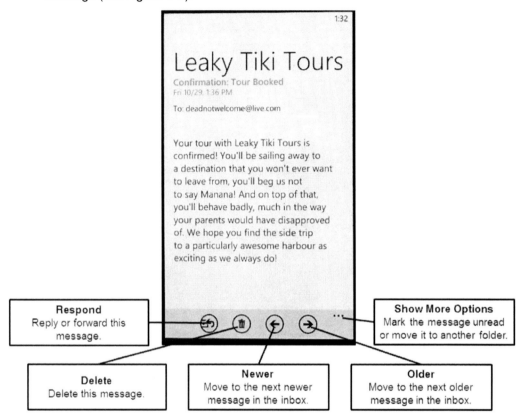

Figure 4–6. *Reading a message.*

7. You can use the buttons at the bottom of the email to **respond** to it (you can reply to all if you have multiple recipients listed) or **forward** it (see Figure 4–7). You can also **delete** it or move between this message and newer or older messages. You can also press the **ellipsis (...)** button to show more options (see Figure 4–8). These additional options let you mark the message as unread or move it to another folder. If you want to return to the message list, press the **back** button.

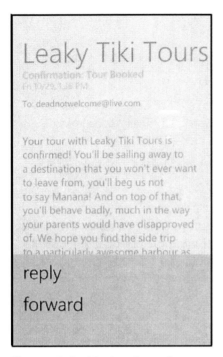

Figure 4–7. *Replying to or forwarding a message.*

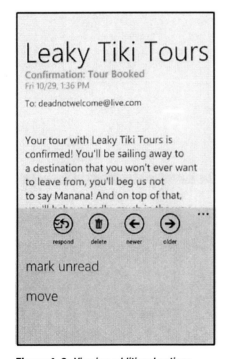

Figure 4–8. *Viewing additional options.*

Composing an Email

Writing a new email message is fast and easy to do. Follow these steps to start composing a message:

1. Turn on and unlock your phone.

2. Tap an inbox (you choices will likely include **Outlook**, **Hotmail**, **Google Mail**, and/or **Yahoo**, among others, depending on the name of the account).

3. You should see a screen similar to the one shown in Figure 4–1. Press the **new** button.

4. A screen similar to the one shown in Figure 4–9 will appear. The first thing you need to do is enter the email address of the person you want to send it to. You can do this one of two ways. First, you can either tap the **+** button in the upper right to select a person from your contacts. Second, you can start typing that person's name (see Figure 4–10), and then choose from the drop-down list of possible matches your phone finds.

Figure 4–9. *Selecting a person from your contacts.*

Figure 4–10. *Entering an email address.*

5. Next, specify a subject for your email. I've chosen a rather simple "hi" as my subject line in Figure 4–11. You'll notice that my Windows Phone 7 device has already put in my signature line. We'll discuss how to change that signature line (or remove it altogether) in the next section.

Figure 4–11. *Entering a subject.*

6. If I would like, I can also change various options regarding my message. As you can see in Figure 4–12, I can attach a picture (by using the **attach** button), set its priority, and/or show lines to add **CC** (carbon copy) and **BCC** (blind carbon copy) recipients (see Figure 4–12). These lines are usually hidden to conserve screen space.

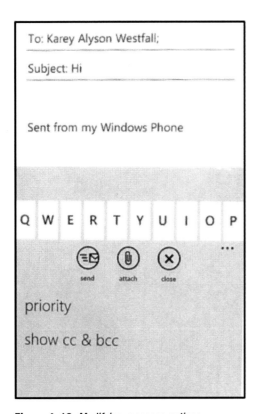

Figure 4–12. *Modifying message options.*

7. Once you finish writing your email, attaching files, and doing whatever else you need do, you can tap the **send** button to get the message on its way (see Figure 4–12). If you decide you don't want to send the message after all, you can tap the **close** or **back** buttons. Tapping **close** brings up three options (see Figure 4–13). The first option lets you **Save** your message in the Drafts folder, which you can access later to resume writing. The second option lets you **Discard** the message, which will cause whatever you've written so far to be deleted. The third option lets you **Cancel** closing the message, returning you to the message so you can either finish it or save it for later.

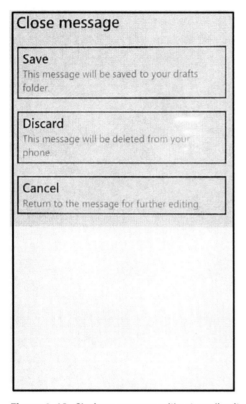

Figure 4–13. *Closing a message without sending it.*

Working With Folders

In the previous example, we discussed moving a message to a different folder. Folders on your phone work much as they do in your normal email program on your computer. You can store messages in them, and your Windows Phone 7 device can open them and display stored messages.

To open a folder, tap the **folders** button (see Figure 4–1) and select the folder you wish to open (see Figure 4–14).

Figure 4–14. *Opening a folder.*

If the folder you want to open isn't listed, click the **show all folders** entry to display the remaining folders (see Figure 4–15). Tap the folder you wish to open. If your phone hasn't downloaded messages from this folder yet, tap **sync this folder**. From this point on, the folder will be synchronized along with your inbox!

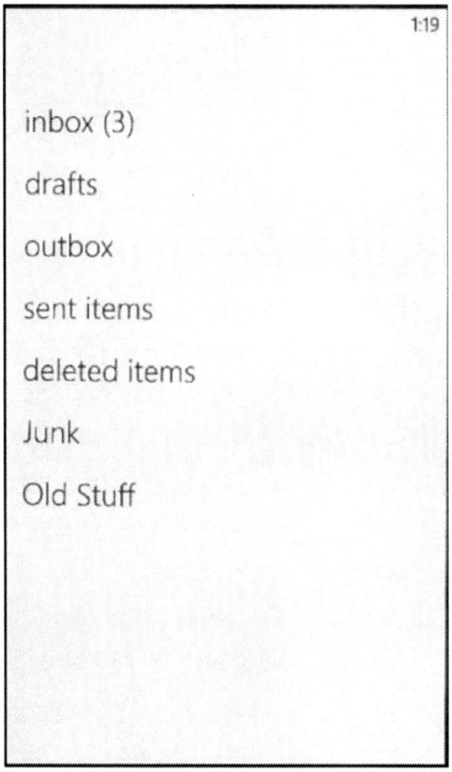

Figure 4–15. *Displaying all your email folders.*

Setting Email Options

The email functions on your phone can be customized by setting a few different options. The steps that follow walk you through and explain these options:

1. Turn on and unlock your phone.

2. Tap an inbox (you choices will likely include **Outlook**, **Hotmail**, **Google Mail**, and/or **Yahoo**, among others, depending on the name of the account).

3. You should see a screen similar to Figure 4–1. Press the **ellipsis (...)** button and choose **settings** (see Figure 4–16).

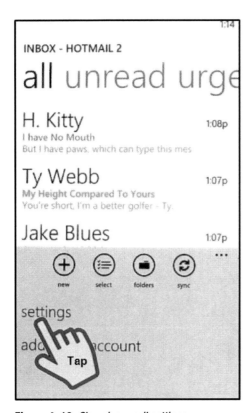

Figure 4–16. *Changing email settings.*

4. The **Settings** screen will appear (see Figure 4–17). From this screen, you can change your sync settings (as you'll see in the next step); always BCC yourself (which is useful if you want to save a copy of your sent messages and your mail server does not provide a copy of sent mail); and change or remove your email signature. To remove your signature, simply uncheck the **Use an email signature** box. To edit your signature, tap the box with your current signature and edit it to your liking.

Figure 4–17. *Changing your sync settings and signature.*

5.   Tapping **sync settings** allows you to modify the synchronization
settings for an account (see Figure 4–18). You can change the name of
the account to something more meaningful, as well as change how
often the phone should check for new messages—**as items arrive** will
cause the phone to synchronize whenever new items are on the server.
(Choosing to sync **as items arrive** provides you with your information as
quickly as possible, but it may also drain your battery more quickly.) You
can also choose how many previous days back your phone should
synchronize messages, as well as what content to synchronize (i.e.,
email, contacts, calendar, or any combination thereof).

Figure 4–18. *Syncing your phone to your computer.*

6. Under normal circumstances, you shouldn't have to change the settings on the lower portion of the screen (see Figure 4–19). However, you may be asked to turn on logging by a technical support person if your phone ever has issues with this account. Otherwise, you can leave it off.

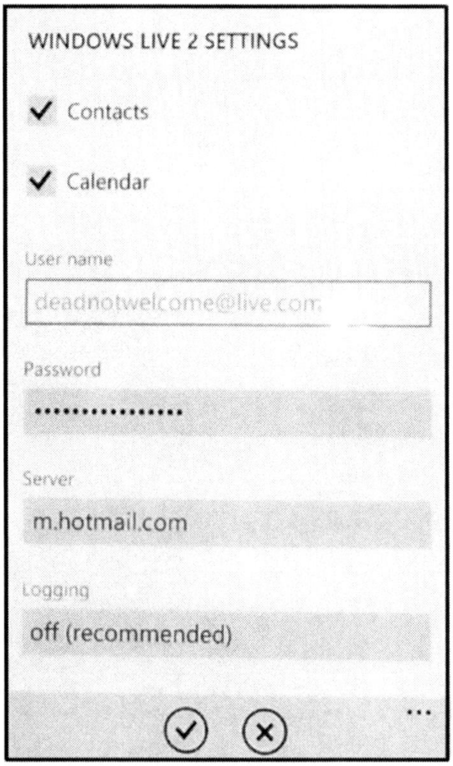

WINDOWS LIVE 2 SETTINGS

✓ Contacts

✓ Calendar

User name

deadnotwelcome@live.com

Password

••••••••••••••••

Server

m.hotmail.com

Logging

off (recommended)

✓   ✗   •••

Figure 4–19. *Changing your email server or turning logging on or off.*

TIP: You can also access sync settings by tapping **settings** in the application list, choosing **email & accounts**, and then tapping the account you wish to modify.

As email becomes increasingly important in daily life, you can be sure that you'll get a lot of use from your Windows Phone 7's inboxes. The interface we've discussed in this chapter should provide a fast and powerful way to manage your messages without feeling like you're in an email overload!

Chapter 5

Setting up and Using Facebook and Twitter

Universally loved or hated (depending on whom you ask), Facebook and Twitter are two services that are always among the most requested on any cellular phone. Microsoft understood this from the start with Windows Phone 7, and it provided integration with Facebook out-of-the-box, without requiring that you install any software. Twitter support is also available through a simple download from the Marketplace. Both services offer a range of ways to communicate with your friends and enemies, as we'll discuss in this chapter!

Adding Your Facebook Account to Your Phone

At the end of Chapter 3, I briefly mentioned that you can add a Facebook account to your phone by following the same steps you use to add email accounts. Please review those steps if you'd like to add a Facebook account to your phone after reading this section (see Figure 3-18 in Chapter 3: "Adding Other Accounts"). The goal of this section is to discuss why you might want to add your Facebook account to the phone, rather than explaining how to download the application (as you would do on an iPhone).

NOTE: To use Facebook on your Windows Phone, you do *not* need to add it to the rest of the phone's accounts (if you follow the steps described in Chapter 3). Instead, you can simply download the application from the Marketplace (see the next section of this chapter). However, if you take this approach, you will miss out on some of the rich experiences the Windows Phone team has built into the phone for Facebook users.

Here are several reasons you might want to add your Facebook login information to the phone:

- **Integration with the People live tile**—Adding your Facebook login information will allow the phone to download recent status updates from your friends under the **What's New** screen in the **People** live tile.

- **Integration with the Pictures live tile**—Adding your Facebook login information will let your phone show recently uploaded Facebook photos to you when you enter the **Pictures** live tile; it will also display your own Facebook photo albums.

- **Integration with your contacts**—Facebook information can be automatically downloaded and matched up with contacts in your phone. This will let you use your phone to access the contact information that people enter into Facebook. You can then tell your phone whether you would like to view the Facebook information for all contacts (**Facebook & contacts** from your email address books) or just for contacts from your email address books. You can change this setting by going to the **applications list**, choosing **settings**, and then swiping to the left to choose **Application** settings. Next, tap **People** and change the setting under the heading, **Include Facebook friends as contacts**.

> **NOTE:** Some people refrain from entering Facebook information into their phone because they're afraid doing so may alter the information for the contacts they have already (e.g., they are afraid that their Windows Live contact photos will be replaced by their contacts' Facebook photos). The Windows Phone team thought about this and designed the phone explicitly *not* to do this. While your phone may show Windows Live, **GMail**, or **Exchange** information alongside Facebook information in the **people** tile, it does *not* merge this information together (i.e., opening up a contact in **Outlook** will not show the Facebook information you see on your phone).

- **Status updates for pinned contacts**—If you choose to pin a person to the **Start** screen (see Chapter 10), and you have this person as a Facebook friend, then her live tile will update automatically to show status updates!

Thus far, we have discussed why you might want to add your Facebook information to your phone. If this sounds interesting, follow the steps in Chapter 3 that describe how to add other accounts. All you need is your Facebook username and password, and you'll be up and running in no time. If you would rather just use the **Facebook** application on your phone, check out the next section.

Downloading and Installing the Facebook Application

While Windows Phone 7 integrates a number of pieces of Facebook information into your phone, it doesn't capture everything. To get the full Facebook mobile experience, follow these steps to download the **Facebook** application from the Marketplace and get it up and running:

1. Turn on and unlock your phone.

2. Tap the **Marketplace** live tile on the **Start** screen (see Figure 5–1).

Figure 5–1. *Accessing the Marketplace.*

3. Press the **search** button on the front of your phone to bring up **Marketplace Search**. Type "Facebook" into the **Search** box and press the **Next** (→) icon on the keyboard.

4. Tap the **Facebook** application (see Figure 5–2).

Figure 5–2. *Searching for the Facebook program.*

5. Tap **Install, allow**, and then **install** to install the application.

6. Once the application is installed, press the **Start** button, then press the **Arrow** icon in the top right to access the **applications list**. Finally, tap the **Facebook** icon to launch the application (see Figure 5–3). Enter your Facebook username and password, then press **login**.

Figure 5–3. *Starting the* **Facebook** *program.*

Using the Facebook Application

There is a lot to explore in the **Facebook** application; the following steps walk you through how to use its main features:

1. After launching the **Facebook** application (see Step 6 in the previous section), you're taken to the main menu (see Figure 5–4). This menu shows your profile picture; your most recent status update; and a list of menu options such as photos, your Facebook inbox, events, friends, and more.

NOTE: Feel free to add me as a Facebook friend, now that you've seen my Facebook page; just make sure to tell me that you read the book in your friend request!

Figure 5–4. *The Facebook app's main menu.*

2. You can scroll down (see Figure 5–5) to check requests, notes, settings, and log out. In practice, you won't need to log out regularly, unless you prefer to for security reasons.

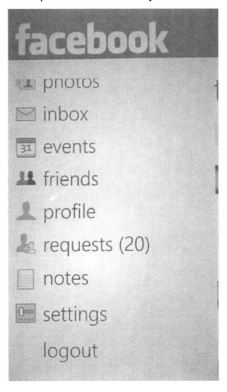

Figure 5–5. *The bottom of the* ***Facebook*** *app's main menu.*

3. Sliding your finger from right to left brings up the **top news** pane (see Figure 5–6), where you can scroll through your friends' status updates and enter one of your own.

Figure 5–6. *The* **Facebook** *app's* **top news** *feed.*

4. Sliding from right to left again shows recent photo albums that your friends have updated (see Figure 5–7).

Figure 5–7. *The **Facebook** app's **photos** pane.*

5. Sliding from right to left yet again displays upcoming events and birthdays (see Figure 5–8).

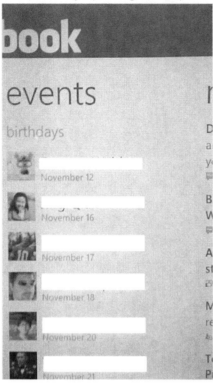

Figure 5–8. *The **Facebook** app's **events** pane.*

6. Finally, sliding from right to left one last time brings up the **notifications** pane (see Figure 5–9). As with the other options, you can scroll through these and tap any one of them to get more information.

Figure 5–9. *The* ***Facebook*** *app's* ***notifications*** *pane.*

As I mentioned previously, there is a lot to explore in the native **Facebook** application. Browse through it, and you'll probably be pleasantly surprised at all you can do without ever needing to get to your computer!

Downloading and Installing the Twitter Application

If Facebook isn't quite your thing (or you just like to use both Twitter and Facebook), you can follow these steps to get started with Twitter on your Windows Phone 7 device:

1. Turn on and unlock your phone.

2. Tap the **Marketplace** live tile on the **Start** screen (see Figure 5–1).

3. Press the **search** button on the front of your phone to bring up **Marketplace Search**. Type "twitter" into the **Search** box and press the **Next** (→) button on the keyboard.

NOTE: More than one program on the Windows Phone Marketplace can access the Twitter service; however, this chapter shows only the official **Twitter** *client.* If you prefer, you can explore other options and choose the one you like best.

4. Tap **Twitter application** (see Figure 5–10) and then press **Install, allow,** and then **install.**

Figure 5–10. *Searching for Twitter.*

5. Once the application is installed, press the **Start** button and then press the **Arrow** icon in the top right to access the **applications list**.

6. Finally, tap the **Twitter** button to launch the application (see Figure 5–11). Press **sign in** and enter your Twitter username (or email) and password.

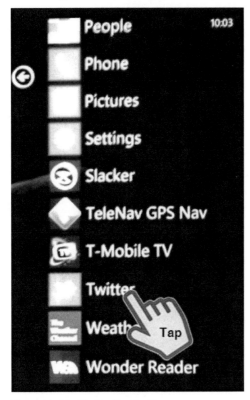

Figure 5–11. *Starting the* **Twitter** *app.*

Using the Twitter Application

Like the **Facebook** application, the **Twitter** application has many areas to explore. However, most of the application is self-explanatory. The main screen of the application appears after you log in (see Figure 5–12). This screen shows your Twitter username at the top and a handful of views.

Figure 5–12. *The **Twitter** app's main screen and menu.*

You can accomplish the following tasks from this screen:

- **Use the buttons at the bottom**—The buttons at the bottom allow you to refresh your current view, compose a Twitter update, send a direct message (DM) to another user, and search for a topic or name.

> **TIP:** Pressing the **search** button also brings up **Top Tweets**, **Trends**, **suggested**, and **nearby** search suggestions. It also brings up your saved searches from www.twitter.com. Swipe your finger from right to left to browse these lists of items after pressing the **search** button.

- **Change settings and profile**—These options are available after pressing the **Ellipsis** button.

■ **Swipe right to left**—Swiping on the main screen from right to left cycles from your Twitter timeline to **mentions**, (direct) **messages**, and **lists**.

> **TIP:** When composing an update, you can attach a photo or insert a friend's username, hashtags, or places—all by clicking the buttons at the bottom and then the **Ellipsis** button. Be sure not to miss these options if you're a power-Twitter user!

If your idea of being social is to use Facebook or Twitter to stay in touch with your friends, colleagues, coworkers, in-laws, family, enemies, children, pets, and/or who/whatever, then Windows Phone 7 has free tools available that can help you do so. And both the Twitter and Facebook services are working on creating live tiles that you'll be able to pin to your **Start** menu. This means you'll always see recent updates at a glance!

Now take a moment before learning about customizing your phone (in the next chapter) and do something social!

Chapter 6

Customizing Your Phone

Windows Phone 7 features an interface that's pretty unique among smartphones, shunning the rows of many icons that are well known to iOS and Android users (and users of Windows Mobile and Pocket PC devices) for large live tiles and a sleek, somewhat sparse, modern design. There are a number of customizations you can make to your phone that can help make it your own, and we'll discuss some of those. Others, like changing your wallpaper on the Lock screen or changing the picture displayed on the Pictures live tile, will be discussed in future chapters.

Re-arranging the Start Screen

Perhaps the first customization you might want to make would be to re-arrange the live tiles on your **Start** screen. This is easily done by pressing and holding a given tile until it becomes highlighted and shows a small pushpin button in the upper right. You can then either drag that item to a new position (the other tiles will re-arrange themselves; see Figure 6–1) or press the pushpin button to remove the tile from your **Start** screen (it will still be available in application list, accessible by pressing the arrow in the upper right of the **Start** screen).

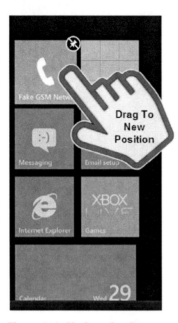

Figure 6–1. *Moving a live tile.*

To take an item from the application list and pin it to the **Start** screen, tap and hold any item until the Pin to **Start** option appears (see Figure 6–2). It will be added to the bottom of the **Start** screen, and you can re-arrange it wherever you wish using the same method just described.

Figure 6–2. *Pinning an item to the start screen.*

Changing the Theme

Blue on black isn't everyone's idea of a good look or inviting interface. Here are the simple steps to customizing your theme options.

1. Turn on your phone and unlock it. Press the arrow in the upper right-hand of the screen to show a list of all options, scroll down, and tap **Settings** (see Figure 6–3).

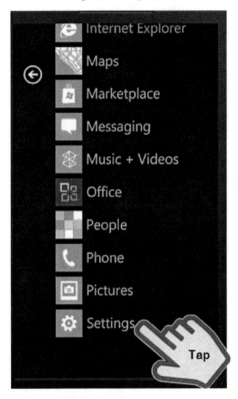

Figure 6–3. *Accessing phone settings.*

2. Tap **Theme** to bring up the theme options (see Figure 6–4).

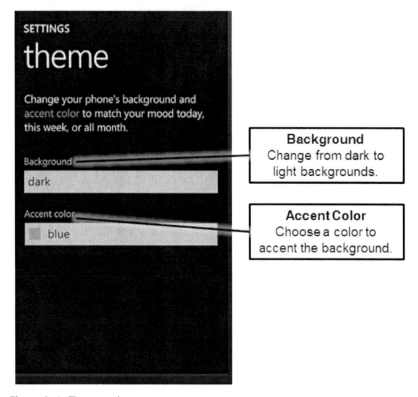

Figure 6–4. *Theme settings.*

3. The first option on this page allows you to change the background from dark (black) to light (white).

> **TIP:** Choosing (or keeping) the background set to "dark" will help conserve battery power!

4. The second option lets you choose between ten "accent" colors. The color you choose here will be the background color of your live tiles on the **Start** screen, and will accent text throughout the phone (e.g., links, bolded text, etc.). Pick one that you like!

5. Once done you can exit out by hitting either the **back** button or the **Windows** button to return directly to the **Start** screen. As you can see from Figure 6–5, I chose a light background with red accent text!

Figure 6–5. *The newly changed theme.*

TIP: Sometimes you might want to play with the accent color and background with an eye for specifically how the Home screen will look. You can quickly see the effect of your choices by changing the setting, hitting the **Windows** key, and then hitting the **back** button to make any additional changes. This saves time by eliminating the need to navigate the settings menu!

NOTE: The icons in the application list that are part of Windows Phone 7 (as opposed to applications you might download from the Marketplace) will change their background color to match your accent color!

Setting the Screen Brightness

Your phone can automatically adjust the brightness of the screen based on the light level around you, or you can set it manually.

1. Turn on your phone and unlock it. Press the arrow in the upper right-hand of the screen to show a list of all options, scroll down, and tap **Settings** (see Figure 6–3).

2. Tap **Brightness**.

3. At the top, you can toggle the Automatically Adjust setting on and off. This setting is useful if you'd like the phone to attempt to adjust the brightness depending on lighting (e.g., brighter in darker lighting conditions, not so bright in bright environments). Sometimes this may not be optimal, though, such as when working outdoors on a sunny day while wearing sunglasses. (Your phone wants to be dim, but you need it brighter to see through the glasses!)

4. Turning Automatically Adjust off lets you manually adjust the level of brightness using the drop-down box below. Change the settings until your screen is at a brightness you find comfortable.

Configuring Ringtones and Sounds

Windows Phone 7 lets you customize your ringtone and other sounds that your phone makes through the **Ringtones and Sounds** settings. (The options are shown in the following list.) To access, open settings (see Step 1 in the section "Changing the Theme"), and tap **Ringtones and Sounds** to bring up a screen similar to Figure 6–6. Figure 6–7 shows the second set of settings visible by scrolling up.

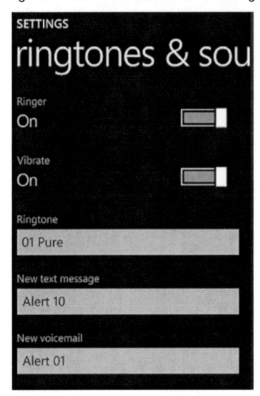

Figure 6–6. *ringtones & sounds settings.*

▓ **Ringer** and **Vibrate**: These two settings toggle on or off the audible ringtone and the vibration function, respectively. You may wish to silence the ringer during a large meeting or other event in which having your phone going off like a banshee would be inappropriate and/or annoying. The vibrate function can also be turned off, for times when you don't wish to be bothered at all, or for those meetings in rooms with nice wooden tables that phones "dance" across when on vibrate! You can also silence your ringer, set it to vibrate, or set it louder by using the volume up or down keys while you're on the **Start** screen (and not playing music) or the Lock screen. Press either key, and then tap the **Ring** icon on the right. If Vibrate is enabled, your phone will go into Vibrate mode. If not, it will simply go into Silent mode. To return to your previous setting, press one of the volume keys again, and tap the **Vibrate** or **Silent** icon.

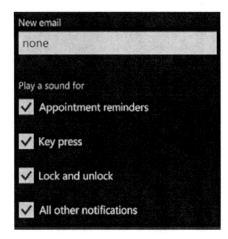

Figure 6–7. *Audio notification settings.*

▓ **Ringtone**: Tapping the gray box will bring up a list of available ringtones. You can preview each one by tapping the **Play** arrow next to the entry (see Figure 6–8). After you're done previewing, tap the tone you want to use.

CHOOSE AN ITEM

01 Pure

Tap

03 Bounce

04 Silk

05 Glide

06 Pearl

07 Shine

Figure 6–8. *Previewing a ringtone.*

- **New Text Message, New voicemail, New email**: These three settings control the sounds made when receiving a text, voicemail, and email. Tapping each one brings up a similar list as the list of ringtones; however, at the top of the list is a "none" option, allowing you to have no sound for that particular notification.

- **Play a sound for…**: Windows Phone 7 can play an audible sound or prompt for appointment reminders (discussed in a future chapter), and each keypress of the keyboard (useful feedback when learning the keyboard and wondering if a key really was pressed!). A sound can also be played for locking/unlocking the phone, as well as other notifications. These are largely personal preferences—do you want a noisy phone or a mostly silent one?

TIP: You can set a custom ringtone for a specific person by going into your **People** live tile, finding the person, and pressing the **edit** button. Then tap **Ringtone**, and select their custom ringer. This is great for callers who you want to have a special ring so you know if you should dash to your phone or let it go to voicemail!

Configuring Keyboard Options

Windows Phone 7 was built to support multiple languages as well as intelligent text entry. The keyboard options, found under the settings menu, and listed below (see Step 1 of "Changing the Theme"), control how the keyboard works, and how the phone handles the text you enter.

Figure 6–9. *Keyboard settings.*

■ **Keyboard Languages**: The Windows Phone 7 keyboard can be configured to cycle through a variety of languages, showing special characters and accent symbols most used in that language. If you don't speak or write in another language often, you may want to tap **Keyboard Languages** and uncheck the boxes next to the languages you do not use. (See Figure 6–10—tap the check mark at the bottom of the screen to save your changes.)

KEYBOARD LANGUAGES

☑ English (United Kingdom)

☑ English (United States)

☑ French (Canada)

☑ French (France)

☑ French (Switzerland)

☑ German (Germany)

Tap

☑

☑

International Sort)

Figure 6–10. *Selecting keyboard languages.*

- **Suggest text and highlight misspelled words**: Windows Phone 7 will attempt to suggest text to you that it thinks you're about to type. Tapping these suggestions will insert the whole word, saving you time. However, if you don't want it to try to suggest things, or highlight what it believes are spelling mistakes, uncheck this box.

- **Correct misspelled words**: Certain words that are commonly misspelled (especially when using an onscreen keyboard) can be corrected automatically. However, if you'd prefer not to have your phone do this, uncheck this box. For individuals in some professions (e.g., medical or technical), this may be essential to prevent "corrections" from confusing your recipients.

- **Insert a space after selecting a suggestion**: Once you've tapped a suggested word, this option determines if the phone will automatically put a space after the word or leave your cursor next to the last letter. Some users may be more comfortable manually adding the space, while others may want to have it done automatically. Uncheck this box to insert spaces manually.

▓ **Insert a period after double-tapping the spacebar**: This option will let you quickly insert a period by double-tapping the spacebar. However, if you often leave multiple blank spaces in text, this feature could become annoying and can be disabled.

▓ **Capitalize the first letter of a sentence**: Windows Phone 7 will automatically capitalize the first letter after you enter a period (to denote the end of a sentence). Uncheck this box if you don't want it to do this.

▓ **Reset text suggestions**: As you enter different words, Windows Phone 7 learns them and will suggest them in the future. If, for whatever reason, you want it to clear its "learned" memory and start from scratch, choose this box. Clearing text suggestions applies only to the text you've entered; the default text suggestions will still be available.

As you can see, Windows Phone 7 provides a number of customization options that can help make your phone your own. We'll learn more as we continue discussing each feature in-depth!

Chapter **7**

Setting up Bluetooth and Wi-Fi

While you may think of your cell phone as only connecting over the air to one place (e.g., your cellular network or the neighborhood cell tower), your Windows Phone 7 device includes both a Bluetooth radio and Wi-Fi radio. Each can be used to improve your experience with the phone, whether through a wireless Bluetooth headset or by connecting to your Wi-Fi network at home to access the Internet faster. In this chapter, we'll cover both of these features and discuss how to configure and use them.

What is Bluetooth?

Named after a long-dead king of Denmark (seriously!), Bluetooth refers to a set of methods that certain devices can use to communicate with each other over a short range. While most of us are familiar with Bluetooth headsets that allow us to stick a small speaker and microphone to the side of our heads and wirelessly communicate with others through our cell phones, Bluetooth is also used to connect keyboards and mice to computers or tablets and to accomplish even more interesting tasks. For example, my best friend recently worked on a project integrating Bluetooth into heart monitoring devices, so that, in the event of a heart attack, the monitor could communicate with the patient's cell phone and notify authorities. In day-to-day use, the monitor could also send heart rate information back to the patient's doctors!

Bluetooth technology, as I mentioned, is restricted to short ranges—to around 30 feet, in most cases. Therefore, it isn't usually used for Internet access, although it can be. For high-speed data networks, you'll connect using Wi-Fi, which we'll discuss later in this chapter.

Turning Bluetooth on and Pairing a Headset

Bluetooth is most often used on cell phones to connect wirelessly to a headset. This allows you to make and receive calls without placing the phone to your ear or using a headset with a cord. While instructions may vary depending on your headset's manufacturer, the following steps should get you up and running in most cases:

1. Turn on your phone and unlock the screen.

2. Tap the **Arrow** button to bring up your list of applications and then tap **Settings** (see Figure 7–1).

Figure 7–1. *Opening phone Settings.*

3. Tap **Bluetooth** (see Figure 7–2).

Figure 7–2. *Accessing your Bluetooth options.*

4. Tap the slider to turn Bluetooth on (see Figure 7–3). Once you do this, the list below the slider will begin to display other available Bluetooth devices. If none are in range, the **Settings** panel will simply say **Searching...** (see Figure 7–4).

Figure 7–3. *Turning Bluetooth on.*

Figure 7–4. *Finding available Bluetooth devices.*

5. This step is the only part that may be different, depending on your headset. You need to consult the manual for your headset to learn how to put the device into *pairing mode*. This is a special mode that allows the phone to find and connect with the headset for the first time. Once your phone is in pairing mode, your Windows Phone 7 device will create a secure connection with the headset. In the future, all you will need to do to use your headset is turn it on. The phone will connect to it automatically!

6. With the headset in pairing mode, your phone should find it quickly and display it in the list of devices nearby (below the **On/Off** slider). If you're in a busy environment, such as on a commuter train, you may see dozens of devices listed. Be careful to find your headset (generally its name will be the same as the brand and model of the headset)! Once you find your headset, tap it (see Figure 7–5).

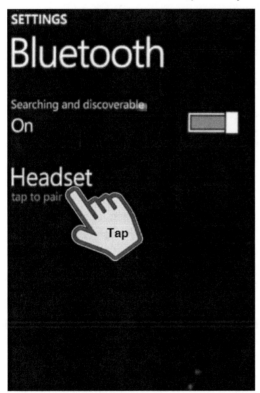

Figure 7–5. *Selecting your headset.*

7. Your phone should connect to your headset automatically and create a secure connection (see Figure 7–6). Most of the time, this does not require you to do anything; however it's possible your phone may ask you for a PIN number or passcode. This passcode can be found in the manual that came with your Bluetooth headset.

Figure 7–6. *Verifying your headset is connected to your phone.*

8. Once the connection has been created, you'll see the **Bluetooth** icon at the top of the screen. This icon indicates that the phone and headset are connected. From this point on, using your headset should be a simple matter of turning it on. Doing so will cause the phone to connect to your headset, as long as you don't turn Bluetooth off. When you finish using the headset, turn it off, and the phone will disconnect from it.

Removing a Paired Device

You may need to remove the secure connection between your phone and headset (known as a *pairing*), especially if you want to switch headsets. To do this, follow these steps:

1. Follow the steps described previously to access your Bluetooth settings.

2. If your old headset or paired device is listed and shown as **connected** below its name, then you need to tap the device to disconnect it.

3. Once the device is disconnected, tap and hold the name of the device until the delete menu appears (see Figure 7–7). Tap **delete** to remove the paired relationship.

Figure 7–7. *Deleting a Bluetooth pairing.*

What is Wi-Fi?

Wi-Fi refers to a special series of protocols (known as IEEE 802.11) that allow devices to join wireless local area networks (WLANs). These protocols (e.g., 802.11b, 802.11g, and 802.11n), transport data over the air, sometimes over great distances. For most people, a single Wi-Fi router (available for around $50) will cover their entire house, providing wireless networking for a range of computers or devices.

On your device, Wi-Fi can be used to connect to the Internet faster than your cellular provider's 3G or 4G network. This can be useful when surfing the web, downloading content from the Marketplace, or just receiving large emails. In some scenarios, one may leave Wi-Fi on all the time, connecting automatically when in range of a wireless network (known as a *hotspot*), and then reverting back to the cellular network connection when out of range. While this provides the fastest possible service, it may also impact the battery life of your device.

Connecting to a Wi-Fi Hotspot

Connecting to your Wi-Fi network is easy with Windows Phone 7. Just follow these steps to do so:

1. Turn on your phone and unlock the screen.

2. Tap the **Arrow** button to bring up your list of applications and then tap **settings** (see Figure 7–1).

3. In the system settings, tap **Wi-Fi** (see Figure 7–8).

Figure 7–8. *Accessing Wi-Fi settings on your phone.*

4. Tap the slider to turn Wi-Fi on (see Figure 7–9). Once you do this, your device will begin finding and displaying a list of available Wi-Fi networks below the slider.

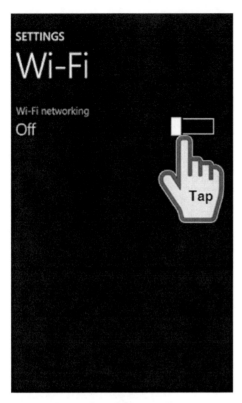

Figure 7–9. *Toggling Wi-Fi on or off.*

NOTE: Your Windows Phone 7 device can only connect to Wi-Fi networks that are visible (or to put it in technical terms, "broadcasting their SSID"). If you've hidden your Wi-Fi network, you'll need to enter your Wi-Fi router's settings and re-enable SSID broadcasting for your phone to connect.

5. Once you find your desired Wi-Fi network, tap it to begin connecting (see Figure 7–10).

Figure 7–10. *Selecting a Wi-Fi network.*

6. If your Wi-Fi network is secured with a password (either through a WEP or WPA key), then you'll be prompted to enter it (see Figure 7–11). You can tap the **show characters** box to show the password, so you know you're entering it correctly.

Figure 7–11. *Entering your whimsical Wi-Fi password.*

7. Assuming you've entered your information correctly, your phone will connect to the Wi-Fi network and show **connected** below the network name on the Wi-Fi settings list (see Figure 7–12). If you have difficulty connecting, it could be due to a temporary issue. You might try turning the Wi-Fi on your device off and back on, and then try to reconnect. Or if you're connecting to a router at home, you might try rebooting the router (by unplugging it and then plugging it back in). You might also need to disable MAC address filtering on your router if you've enabled it.

Figure 7–12. *Verifying a Wi-Fi connection.*

Changing Advanced Wi-Fi Settings and Removing Networks

Most Wi-Fi networks are set up so that connecting is easy and simple. However, certain networks—and this is particularly true of corporate secured networks—may require you to use different settings, such as proxy server configuration, before you can connect to them. Follow these steps to enter the Advanced Wi-Fi settings, entering any values your network administrator may provide:

1. Turn on your phone and unlock the screen.

2. Tap the **Arrow** button to bring up your list of applications and then tap **settings** (see Figure 7–1).

3. Tap **Wi-Fi** (see Figure 7–8).

4. Tap and hold on the name of the Wi-Fi network you want to configure. If you haven't connected to this network before, you may be prompted for a password. If you are connected, then you'll see a screen similar to the one shown in Figure 7–13.

Figure 7–13. *Editing Wi-Fi settings.*

5. Tap **delete** to remove the network if you no longer wish to connect to it. If you need to specify advanced settings, tap **edit**, and a screen similar to the one shown in Figure 7–14 will appear.

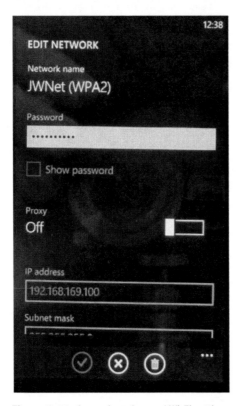

Figure 7–14. *Accessing advanced Wi-Fi settings.*

6. The top of the **Edit Network** screen lists the network name (SSID) and your saved network password. If you've been given the network address and the port of a proxy server to connect to, tap the **Proxy** checkbox to bring up its settings (see Figure 7–15).

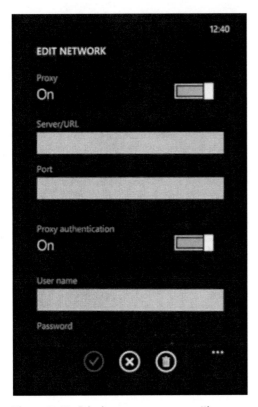

Figure 7–15. *Bringing up proxy server settings.*

7. If your proxy server requires authentication, tap the **Proxy authentication** checkbox and enter your username and password.

8. Below the proxy settings, you can find a few network connection details that your system administrator may need if you have trouble accessing the network. These details include your IP address, Gateway, DNS, and Subnet mask (see Figure 7–16).

Figure 7–16. *Modifying your network settings.*

9. If you make any changes that you'd like to save, tap the **Checkmark** icon or **Accept** button at the bottom. To cancel any changes, tap the **x** or **Cancel** button. If you'd like to delete this network, whether to stop connecting to it or so you can reconfigure it later, then tap the **Delete** button, which has a nice little **Trashcan** icon.

> **NOTE:** Certain Wi-Fi networks may require you to authenticate yourself by means of a special certificate file. This file may be loaded on to your device by attaching the .CER file to a self-addressed email message, and then opening the email on your device and tapping the certificate to add it to your device's certificate storage!

Wi-Fi networks and Bluetooth devices allow us to connect to the world around us with our phones, perhaps more intimately than the regular old cellular network (since our routers generally are closer). While this doesn't mean you'll have a better relationship with your headset than your cell tower, it does mean that you'll have easier ways to communicate with the actual people you have intimate relationships with—and in some cases (e.g., states where you are legally not allowed to hold a cell phone while driving), you can stay connected and not break the law by using your headset while driving!

Chapter 8

Managing and Securing Your Phone

Our Windows Phone 7 devices represent only a small subset of all the information we keep, yet this is usually the most important subset we have—it holds all of our friends' contact information; our email; our favorite music; our photos; and for dedicated gamers, even our Xbox avatar! It's important, therefore, that we be able to manage our phones and keep the information safe. In this chapter, we'll discuss securing our phones with a password, managing our phones with Windows Live, and remotely disabling or wiping data from our phones in case they get lost!

> **NOTE:** Many of the features we will discuss in this chapter require you to have added at least one Windows Live account to your phone (see Chapter 3: "Setting up Accounts" for more information on adding a Windows Live account). If you choose not to add a Windows Live account, the only features discussed in this chapter that you'll be able to use are the tips for setting the lock screen password and time-out interval.

Setting the Lock Screen Wallpaper and Password

Your **lock** screen can be customized to have your own special wallpaper and require a four-digit password to be entered in order to use the phone. Follow these steps to configure your **lock** screen:

1. Turn on and unlock your phone.

2. Tap the **Arrow** icon in the upper right of the screen to bring up the list of applications. At the bottom of the list, tap **settings** (see Figure 8–1).

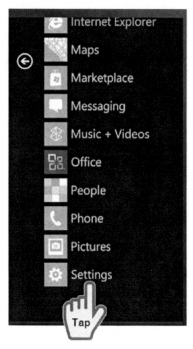

Figure 8–1. *Accessing your phone's settings.*

3. Tap **lock & wallpaper** (see Figure 8–2).

Figure 8–2. *Accessing your **lock & wallpaper** settings.*

4. To change the wallpaper on the **lock** screen, tap the **change wallpaper** button (see Figure 8–3). This will bring up the standard picture chooser, letting you select an image from your camera roll or from any other photos you have access to on your device.

Figure 8–3. *Changing the wallpaper on the* ***lock*** *screen.*

5. In this example, you will need to choose an image as your wallpaper (see Figure 8–4).

Figure 8–4. *Navigating to a wallpaper image.*

6. After you select an image as your wallpaper (see Figure 8–5), your phone lets you crop the picture if you so desire. In the example shown, the picture is nicely cropped already, so you could just hit the **crop** button at the bottom without making any changes (see Figure 8–6).

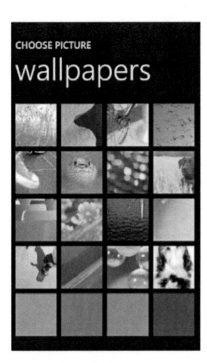

Figure 8–5. *Selecting an image as your wallpaper.*

Figure 8–6. *Cropping a photo.*

7. The phone now takes you back to the **lock & wallpaper** options (see Figure 8–2). From here, you can now set the screen time-out interval. This option controls how long the phone's screen will remain turned on after you stop using it. This is helpful in case you forget to turn your phone off; however, in some cases you may want to set the time-out interval higher or disable it altogether (especially if you're reading documents). Figure 8–7 shows your options; simply select whichever option works best for you.

Figure 8–7. *Choosing your time-out interval.*

NOTE: If you decide to enable a password, the **never** option will be removed from the list of time-out options.

8. To set a four-digit password, tap the **On/Off** slider (see Figure 8–8).

Figure 8–8. *Adding a password to your time-out screen.*

9. In the box that appears (see Figure 8–9), set a four-digit password that's easy for you to remember, but hard for others to guess. Ideally, you want to set a number that would take five or more tries for someone to guess. This excludes passwords like "1234" or "1111" and so on. When you're satisfied with your choice, press **done**.

Figure 8–9. *Entering a four-digit password.*

NOTE: If you forget your password, you're given five tries to enter it. After that, your phone begins to delay how often you can try unlocking it, first by one minute, then two, then four, and so forth, doubling the interval between each successive wrong entry. This way, someone who obtains your phone can't easily try all 10,000 possible combinations in a short amount of time to "get in." Be careful, though—these delays remain even if you turn off and remove the battery from your phone!

10. You've now set your password, and your phone will prompt you for it each time you turn it on and unlock it.

Using Windows Live To Find Your Phone

All of us, at one time or another, misplace something. For some of us, it's not a big deal (maybe it was just a pen!); for others, it may be a big problem (e.g., keys, wallets, phones, or nuclear launch codes). Thankfully, your Windows Phone 7 device give you a suite of tools that will help you find a lost phone. We'll begin by discussing how to configure those options on your phone, and then move onto showing you how to use them through your computer. Follow these steps to do so:

1. Turn on and unlock your phone.

2. Tap the **Arrow** icon in the upper right of the screen to bring up the list of applications. At the bottom of the list, tap **settings** (see Figure 8–1).

3. Tap **find my phone** (see Figure 8–10).

Figure 8–10. *Setting up the **find my phone** feature.*

4. The **find my phone** settings will appear (see Figure 8–11). While the basic features described on this screen (e.g., map, ring, lock, or erase) will work without the boxes on this screen being checked, they'll tend to work faster if you decide to go ahead and check both boxes. The first box, **Save my location periodically for better mapping**, periodically saves your phone's location to a central server. Consequently, if you're looking for your phone, you can find the general area it is in faster. The second box, **Get results faster (may use more battery)**, controls whether the phone should periodically send additional information to Windows Live servers that would aid in finding your phone. It will use a bit more battery power than if you leave this option turned off. However, if you charge frequently and/or are a bit forgetful and/or live in a high crime area, this option might be worth turning on!

Figure 8–11. *Improving the speed and accuracy of the **find my phone** feature.*

5. Once you're done setting these options on your phone, you can turn it off and set it aside for a few moments. Meanwhile, we'll explore how to use the Windows Live phone website to find your phone.

6. Begin by opening a web browser on your computer and going to `http://windowsphone.live.com`.

7. On the **sign in** screen (see Figure 8–12), enter your Windows Live ID and password.

Figure 8–12. *Signing in to Windows Live.*

8. You'll then be taken to the Windows Phone site, which will show information specific to your phone, including photos you've taken and uploaded, your contacts, your OneNote notebooks, and more. You can explore this website later—for now, we'll just discuss the options listed under **FIND MY PHONE** (see Figure 8–13).

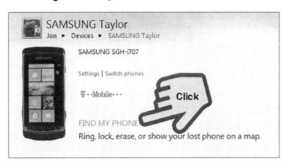

Figure 8–13. *Exploring options for **FIND MY PHONE**.*

9. You're given four options to help you find your phone: **Map It**, which shows you the approximate location of the phone; **Ring It**, which makes it ring loudly so you can find it; **Lock It**, which enables you to prevent access to the phone in case you haven't set a password; and **Erase It**, which lets you wipe all your personal data if the phone has been stolen. We'll walk through each of these options in the steps that follow.

10. Clicking **Map It** will first display an approximate location based on where your phone last reported its location (see Figure 8–14).

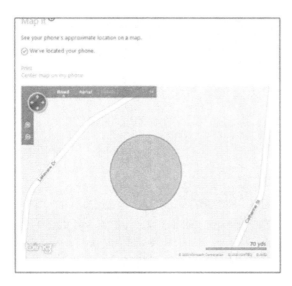

Figure 8–14. *Mapping your phone's last reported location.*

11. If the **Map It** feature doesn't help you much, then you might try the **Ring It** feature. When you activate this feature, your phone will ring with a distinctive ring tone (you can preview this ring tone on your PC, so you know what it will sound like) at the phone's loudest setting. Once you see a confirmation that the ring request has been sent (see Figure 8–15), you can begin listening. Normally, it takes between 10-20 seconds for the ringing to start; it will stop once you find the device and press the power button.

Figure 8–15. *Finding your phone with the **Ring It** feature.*

12. If the **Ring It** feature doesn't help you find your phone, then alas, it might not be physically nearby. At this point, you can use the **Lock It** feature to cause the phone to display a special message, perhaps asking some kind person to send you your phone or otherwise contact you (see Figure 8–16 for an example of what you might say). You can also have the phone ring at the same time by checking the **Ring your phone** box, as shown in Figure 8–16; this alerts any nearby person to its presence.

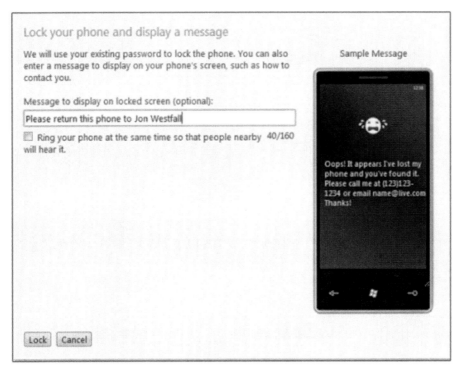

Figure 8–16. *Locking your phone and displaying a message.*

13. If all else fails—and you're pretty sure your device has been stolen or lost for good—then you'll probably want to wipe your phone. This will remove all of your personal data, returning your phone to the way it was when you removed it from the box. To begin this process, click **Wipe It**.

14. A dialog box will appear, requiring that you confirm that you want to send the wipe signal (see Figure 8–17). Once you send the signal, the phone will lock, and the wipe process will begin.

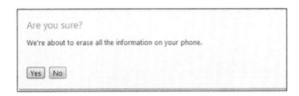

Figure 8–17. *Confirming that you want to wipe your phone.*

15. Once wiped, the **FIND MY PHONE** section of the Windows Phone website will show a message similar to the one shown in Figure 8–18. This message will persist until you get the phone back and reconfigure your Windows Live account on it.

⊘ Your phone was erased on 11/1/2010 at 8:18 PM
We've reset your phone to the factory settings and erased all the information on it.

We suggest that you contact your mobile operator to make sure that nobody can make calls from your phone.

Go back to summary page

CAUTION: If you send a **Wipe It** request to your phone and then find it, you will be unable to stop the wipe, even if you unlock your phone before it begins!

NOTE: If your phone is wiped, any data on it is deleted permenantly. Many things, however, such as uploaded SkyDrive photos and email, are not lost as they are stored on the internet. However if you do not synchronize photos to your computer using the Zune software, and do not synchronize to SkyDrive, these will be lost. Therefore, you may want to make sure important information on your phone is either synchronized to the Internet, or periodically backed up in some way manually (e.g., by emailing files to yourself, using the Zune software, etc...)

Chapter **9**

Searching Your Phone and Using Speech

One of the goals of the team that built Windows Phone 7 was to make finding information as easy and quick as possible. The team knew that, for most information, people do not want to be moving through apps, menus, buttons, and who knows what else—they just want to find the information ASAP! For that reason, the team dedicated an entire button on the device to searching: the **search** button.

Understanding the Search Button

If you've used any previous version of Windows Mobile, then you know that the operating system underpinning it was radically re-created in Windows Phone 7. You also know that prior versions of Windows Mobile had a search capability that wasn't as useful as it sounded. Like the **Search** feature in Windows XP, it took time to complete, and it didn't always behave as expected. The **Search** feature in Windows Phone 7 is different; it behaves much like the **Search** feature on a Windows Vista or Windows 7 machine. Follow these steps to access and use the **Search** feature on your Windows Phone 7 device:

1. The **search** button is your first line of attack for many information-seeking activities. To initiate a search, turn on and unlock your phone.

2. Press the **search** button. If this is the first time you've searched for something, you may get a message asking whether it is OK for the **Search** feature to use your physical location data to aid in its searches. If you do not turn this feature on, you won't be able to get local search information.

Figure 9–1. *Allowing the **Search** feature to use your location.*

3. After accepting or declining the request to use your physical location, you'll get a screen similar to the one shown in Figure 9–2, with a background by Microsoft Bing. You're now ready to start searching.

Tap here to enter your search.

Activate speech search.

Get info on the background picture.

Find out who created this picture.

Figure 9–2. *The Bing Search screen.*

4.   You'll notice some interesting things about the **Search** box shown in Figure 9–2. First, the graphic has two small areas that have darkened rectangles. If tapped on, they provide information about the graphic, a nice touch if you're curious about what you're looking at. In the case of the screenshot shown in Figure 9–3, Bing teases us by not telling us the name of the bird.

Figure 9–3. *Bing tells us more about this bird!*

Of course, you could just tap the image, and Bing would search for the name of the bird and bring back some results. In this way, you could perform your first search without really trying!

Understanding Web Search Results

The search results on the *Western Crowned Pigeon* highlight the three types of searches Bing can provide for you on your phone:

Figure 9–4. *Viewing search results.*

Web—The results on this pane show web pages that may be of interest to you as you search for information. It also shows one or two sponsored sites that may be of interest, or may be easily skipped.

Figure 9–5. *Local search results.*

Local—The results here show anything nearby that matches the search term. Presumably there are no Western Crowned Pigeon breeders in the area of Manhattan, so the results sadly come up empty.

Figure 9–6. *News results.*

News—Shockingly, there are no news stories pertaining to our feathered friend. However, it's easy to compose a search that will retrieve some news about a given search subject, as shown in Figure 9–7. Tapping a story will take you to the web page, so you can read the entire article in all its shocking detail (see Figure 9–8).

Figure 9–7. *News results showing stories.*

Figure 9–8. *A news article found by Bing.*

Using Speech

Windows Phone 7 even allows you to search the Web using your voice to enter your query (as opposed to typing it in). To access this feature, follow these steps:

1. Turn on and unlock your phone.

2. Press the **search** button.

3. Tap the **Microphone** icon at the end of the **Search** box (see Figure 9–9).

Figure 9–9. *Accessing speech-based searches.*

4. When the **Listening** box appears (see Figure 9–10), say whatever you want to search for, taking care to enunciate clearly. Your phone will attempt to match what you are saying to words that it knows, and then start the search.

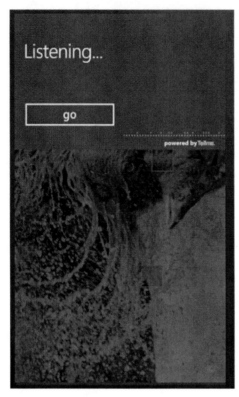

Figure 9–10. *Listening for your input.*

5. If your phone cannot hear you, you'll receive an error similar to the one shown in Figure 9–11. If this happens, tap the **speak** button and try searching again. In loud environments, the voice-based **Search** feature might not be able to distinguish what you are saying from ambient noises, so you may wish to enter your search on the keyboard if you're in a crowd. If your phone cannot understand what you've said, it will raise an error; in this case, you can try again by pressing the **speak** button.

NOTE: A Wi-Fi or cellular data connection is required to use speech recognition.

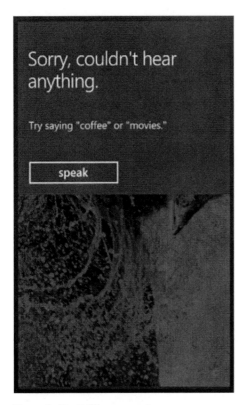

Figure 9–11. *Raising a speech error.*

NOTE: Searching by voice isn't the only thing you can tell your phone to do. Your Windows Phone 7 device can also complete simple voice-directed tasks. To see this in action, hold the **Windows** button down on the front of your device and say this phrase when the **Listening** box appears: "What can I say" (see Figure 9–12).

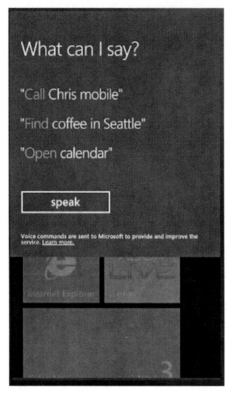

Figure 9–12. *Examples of what you can say to the speech-recognition engine.*

Customizing Search Settings

You can customize how Bing search operates by accessing and configuring the search settings. Follow these steps to do so:

1. Turn on and unlock your phone.

2. Press the **Arrow** icon in the upper right and tap **Settings**.

3. Press the upper part of the screen and slide your finger to the left to access the **Applications** settings (see Figure 9–13).

Figure 9–13. *Accessing the* ***Applications*** *settings.*

4. Tap **Search** (see Figure 9–14).

Figure 9–14. *Changing the Search settings.*

5. A screen similar to the one shown in Figure 9–15 will appear. From this screen, you can tell your phone whether to use your location when conducting searches, whether to turn on the Bing suggestions your phone provides while you are typing a search query, and whether to delete your **Search** history. You can also view the Windows Phone Privacy statement.

Figure 9–15. *The Search settings.*

Searching for Your Information

Windows Phone 7 also features a contextual search option within several live tiles and applications. For example, opening up the **People** live tile and then pressing the **search** button will allow you to search for a person in your contacts. Similarly, opening up an email account and pressing the **search** button will allow you to search the inbox of that account for specific messages that match your query. The following live tiles and applications feature context-specific searches, while pressing the **search** button in other areas of the phone will merely open Bing and allow you to search the Web.

- The **People** live tile search will find names that match your query.

- Email accounts allow you to search for parts of a message.

- The Marketplace features a search for applications or other content (such as music); you can access this information by pressing the **search** button.

- Marketplace Search can also be accessed by pressing the **search** button from within the **Music and Videos** live tile or the **Zune** media player application.

- The **Phone** live tile allows you to press the **search** button and search the call history.

- Pressing the **search** button in the **Maps** application actually launches Bing search, which might catch you by surprise. To search within **Maps**, you must tap the **Search** icon on the bottom menu bar (see Chapter 22: "Using Maps" for more information on how to use the **Maps** application).

Chapter 10

Connecting With People: Using the People Live Tile

Most phones provide an address book feature that allows you to view information on each person you've entered, create new entries, and perhaps do a few quick actions such as dialing a person's number. Windows Phone 7 provides the **People** live tile, which lets you perform all of these action and quite a few more. We'll explore this live tile in depth in this chapter, including how to use it to manage all the information for those people that matter most to you!

Adding a Person to Your Contacts

It's not hard to add a person to your contacts in Windows Phone 7; however, there are a plethora of options you can choose from during the process. The following steps walk you through adding a contact and selecting from the available options:

1. Turn on your phone and unlock it.

2. Press the **People** live tile. You should see a screen similar to the one shown in Figure 10–1.

Figure 10–1. *Accessing your list of contacts.*

3. Tap the **New** button and a screen similar to the one shown in Figure 10–2 will appear.

Save
Save the information to your contacts.

Cancel
Do not save, exit and discard the information entered.

Figure 10–2. *The New Contact screen.*

4. The **New Contact** screen displays a number of subsections, each with an **Add** (+) button next to it. This screen lets you add different types of information quickly and easily, without having to scroll through the many available options.

5. Tap the **Add** button next to **Name** to begin entering the name of a new contact (see Figure 10–3). Fields exist for **First name**, **Last name**, **Company**, **Middle name**, **Nickname**, **Title**, and **Suffix**. When you're finished adding a contact, press the **Accept** button (which resembles a checkmark); or, if you're not happy with your changes, press the **Reject** button (which resembles the letter "x"). Assuming you accept your changes, you'll see the information for the contact show up on his **Profile** screen.

Figure 10–3. *Editing a contact's name.*

6. Now that the information has appeared (see Figure 10–4), you can continue by tapping the **Add** button next to any information you have for the person you want to store, including phone numbers (work, mobile, home, home 2, work 2, company, pager, home fax, and work fax); email addresses (work, personal, and other); and other information (including his address, website, birthday, notes, anniversary, significant other, children, office location, and job title).

Figure 10–4. *The newly edited name appears on the **New Contact** screen.*

7. You can also tap the **Add** button next to **ringtone** and choose a custom ringtone for this contact; this enables you to know when he's calling just by the sound the phone makes!

> **NOTE:** Certain manufacturers or cellular providers may add or remove ringtones to make their phones more unique (e.g., adding the T-Mobile jingle). Thus your list of ringtones might include more or fewer options than the Windows Phone 7 device of a friend or co-worker.

8. Finally, you can also add a photo of the person, whether it's one you've taken previously or one that you have stored somewhere your phone can access it. To do this, tap **add photo** and select from the **Choose Picture** screen (see Figure 10–5). You can also tap the **Camera** button at the bottom of this screen to launch your camera, and then snap a picture of the person right now (probably much to his chagrin).

Figure 10–5. *Choosing a photo.*

9. Once you're done, tap the **Save** button (see Figure 10–6). Your new contact will now appear in the **People** live tile, along with everyone else!

Figure 10–6. *Saving the new contact.*

Browsing, Editing, and Linking Your Contacts

It's easy to browse and edit contacts. You can also link contacts that you may have listed under different names, depending on the service in question. For example, my brother-in-law appears with his full name in my contacts list; however, on Facebook he only uses his first and middle names. Follow these steps to link a contact's multiple accounts together:

1. Turn on your phone and unlock it.

2. Press the **People** live tile. You should see a screen similar to the one shown in Figure 10–1. Your **Contacts** screen will appear (see Figure 10–7).

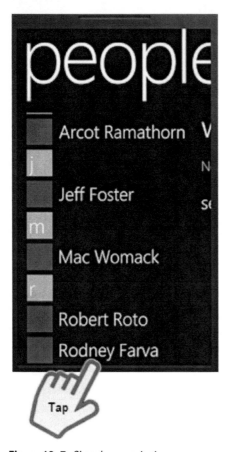

Figure 10–7. *Choosing a contact.*

　　3.　Tap the name of the person you would like to view (see Figure 10–8).

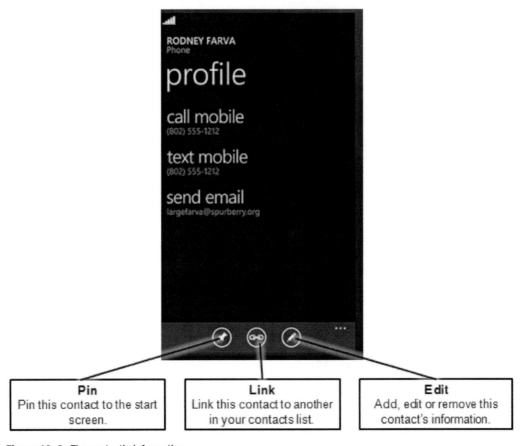

Figure 10–8. *The contact's information.*

4. Tap the **Link** button to link this contact to another on your phone (see Figure 10–8). Note that your phone will keep all the contact's information under one record and prevent duplicates.

5. A screen similar to the one shown in Figure 10–9 will appear. Tap **choose a contact** to find the other contact record for this person. Tap that person's name, and the contacts will become linked.

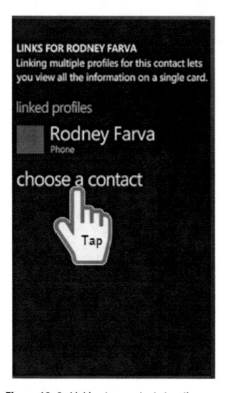

Figure 10–9. *Linking two contacts together.*

6. To edit a contact, tap the **Edit** button (see Figure 10–8). A screen similar to the one shown in Figure 10–10 will appear.

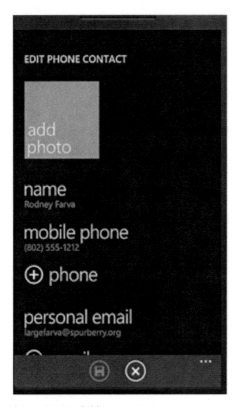

Figure 10–10. *Editing a contact.*

7. Let's assume you'd like to add another email address for this person. Scroll up and press the **Add** (+) button next to **email** (see Figure 10–11).

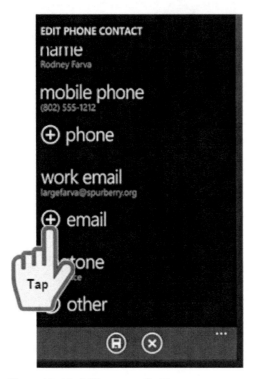

Figure 10–11. *Adding an email address.*

8. Now add the person's new email address; optionally, you can change the email address type from **personal** to **business** or **other** (see Figure 10–12). When you're done, tap the **Accept** checkmark at the bottom to save your changes.

Figure 10–12. *Editing or entering an email address.*

9. The information is now updated in the person's **Contact** screen (see Figure 10–13).

TIP: Linking a person's accounts together may cause you to see a contact photo from her Facebook or Windows Live account, as opposed to the photo you'd prefer to use for her. To choose a photo to see, edit the contact and tap the photo—you'll be given a list of that contact's photos to select from!

Figure 10–13. *The new email address appears in the contact's information.*

Pinning and Deleting

Obviously, you interact with some contacts more than others. For those people you interact with frequently, you might want to put this information somewhere special, such as the **Start** screen. You may also need to remove a contact from time-to-time. The following steps explore how to pin a contact to the **Start** menu, unpin a contact from the **Start** menu, and remove a contact completely from your list of contacts:

1.   Turn on your phone and unlock it.

2.   Press the **People** live tile. You should see a screen similar to the one shown in Figure 10–1.

3.   Find the contact you wish to pin to the **Start** screen, then press and hold on that person's name until the menu shown in Figure 10–14 appears.

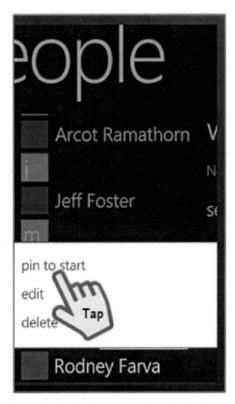

Figure 10–14. *Pinning a contact to the **Start** menu.*

4. After returning to your **Start** screen, you should see the person's name appear in a live tile. If you've given the person a picture, or have this person as a Facebook contact, then the person's picture will appear, as well (see Figure 10–15).

Figure 10–15. *The contact is now pinned to the **Start** screen.*

5. If you want to remove this person from your **Start** screen, press and hold the tile down until it is highlighted and has an **Unpin** icon in the upper right (see Figure 10–16). Tap that icon to remove the person's tile. Remember: This does *not* delete the person from your contacts; it simply removes the person's tile from the **Start** screen.

Figure 10–16. *Unpinning a contact.*

6. You can delete a contact in one of two ways. First, you can follow steps to select a contact and then tap **Delete**. Second, you can delete a contact as you view it by pressing the **Ellipsis** button and choosing **delete** (see Figure 10–17).

Figure 10–17. *Deleting a contact.*

Finding Out What's New!

Windows Phone 7 integrates information from Facebook and Windows Live into the **what's new** screen of the **People** live tile. Follow these steps to see these updates:

1. Turn on your phone and unlock it.

2. Press the **People** live tile. You should see a screen similar to the one shown in Figure 10–1.

3. Press and slide the screen to the left to bring up the **what's new** screen (see Figure 10–18).

Figure 10–18. *Finding out what is new with your contacts through the **what's new** pane.*

4. You can scroll down the list to see all entries. If you scroll all the way to the bottom, then you can tap **get older posts** to see even more posts (see Figure 10–19).

Figure 10–19. *Getting status updates that are older than the ones listed.*

5. Finally, tapping the **Word bubble** to the right of the status update will let you comment directly on it. Or you can simply "like" the update by pressing the **like** button (see Figure 10–20).

Figure 10–20. *Commenting on or "liking" a status update.*

Windows Phone 7 makes it easy to access and keep together different pieces of information about a given person. Linking contacts together from sources such as Facebook and Windows Live can give you a better picture of one person. And by pinning a contact to the **Start** screen, you can be sure you'll never overlook someone important or have trouble finding her in an emergency!

Chapter 11

Setting Alarms and Reminders

It happens to the best of us. You're swamped at the office, or perhaps the kids are causing you to run around like a mad person; and before you know it, you've forgotten to do something. If only that magical device you carry to make phone calls could help you out by reminding you about important events. Thankfully, it can! In this chapter, we'll talk about the various ways your phone can alert you to important events through alarms and reminders.

Setting an Alarm

Setting an alarm using Windows Phone 7 is simple; however, there are options you may want to consider when setting an alarm.

> **NOTE:** I'm a big believer in testing your alarm before using it to wake you up in the morning. Some of us are heavier sleepers than others, and some alarm tones work better than others. The first night with a new alarm tone/volume, I always set one other alarm-type device, such as an alarm clock, just to be safe!

To get started, turn on your device and unlock it. You should be at the **Start** screen. If not, press the **Windows** key to return to it. Follow these steps to set an alarm:

1. Click the **Arrow** icon in the upper right to show all of your applications (see Figure 11–1).

Figure 11–1. *Your phone's* ***start*** *screen, accessing the* ***applications*** *list.*

2. Tap **Alarms** (see Figure 11–2).

Figure 11–2. *Tapping* ***Alarms*** *lets you set or edit alarms.*

3. You should see a screen similar to the one shown in Figure 11–3; however, if you haven't set any alarms yet, it will read **no saved alarms**. You can enable or disable saved alarms on this screen by pressing the **Toggle** button on the right. Tapping this button will slide the switch to the right (enabled) or left (disabled).

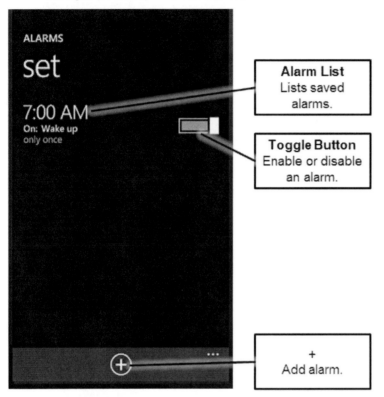

Figure 11–3. *The Alarm list.*

4. Tap **Add** (see Figure 11–4).

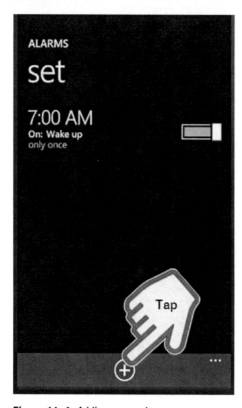

Figure 11–4. *Adding a new alarm.*

5. A screen similar to the one shown in Figure 11–5 will appear. You can then tap each element to adjust it. You can also set the time, what days the alarm should repeat on (see Figure 11–6), the sound you want to have played, and the name of the alarm (which will show up in the list shown in Figure 11–3).

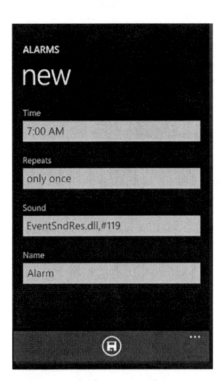

Figure 11–5. *Setting alarm options.*

Figure 11–6. *Choosing the days the alarm should sound on.*

Setting a Calendar Reminder

We'll discuss the calendar in more detail in the next chapter. However, if you simply want to create a reminder for a calendar entry, follow these quick and easy steps:

1.   From the **Home** screen, tap the **Calendar** live tile.

2.   You should see a grid view similar to the one shown in Figure 11–7. Find the appointment you want to add the reminder for and tap it (see Figure 11–7). If you need help finding appointments or adding them, see Chapter 12: "Using & Customizing your Calendar."

Figure 11–7. *Tapping on a calendar appointment.*

3.   Tapping the calendar appointment brings up the **Details** screen, tap the **Edit** button to add the reminder (see Figure 11–8).

Figure 11–8. *Editing a calendar appointment.*

4.   Tap **more details** (see Figure 11–9).

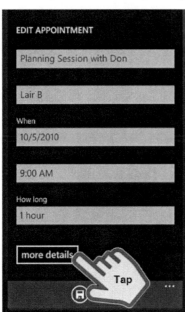

Figure 11–9. *Specifying more details on an appointment.*

5. Tap the **Reminder** box (see Figure 11–10) and select a time for the reminder. Most times are close to the appointment, such as 5 minutes or 15 minutes; however, you can also see a few longer intervals, such as 1 day or 1 week (see Figure 11–11).

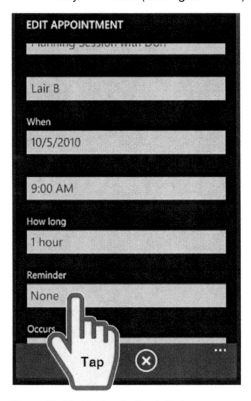

Figure 11–10. *Tapping the Reminder box.*

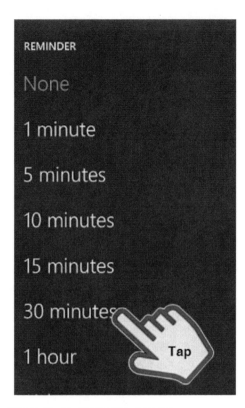

Figure 11–11. *Setting the reminder.*

6. When done, hit the **Save** button (see Figure 11–12). You'll be taken back to the grid-based **Day** view of your calendar and the reminder will be set. You can verify this by tapping the appointment once more—you'll see the reminder displayed on the **Details** screen.

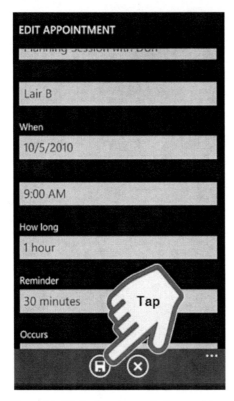

Figure 11–12. *Saving changes to the appointment.*

Setting up Calendar Reminders Online

If you use **Windows Live Calendar, Outlook**, or **Google Calendar** to manage your schedule, and you have added those accounts to your Windows Phone 7 device, then you can add reminders online that will also be set on your phone. This can be helpful for multiple events that you might need to add reminders for. Follow the brief steps outlined for each of the services you want to set reminders for:

- **Windows Live Calendar (Hotmail)**—Bring up your calendar and hover over the entry you want to add a reminder for (see Figure 11–13). Click **Edit Event**, choose your preferred reminder duration, and then press **Save**.

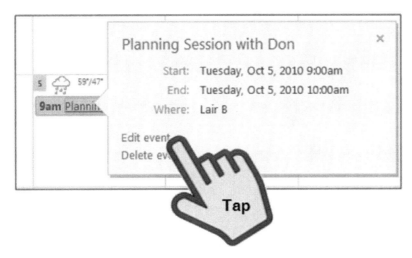

Figure 11–13. *Editing an appointment.*

- **Outlook**—Click the desired calendar appointment you want to add the reminder for and change the **Reminder** entry in the **Options** area of the ribbon toolbar (see Figure 11–14).

Figure 11–14. *Setting a Reminder in Outlook.*

- **Google Calendar**—Click the desired calendar appointment and choose **edit event details**. Next, click **Add Reminder** on the **Edit** screen and choose **Pop-Up** (see Figure 11–15).

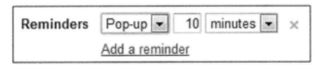

Figure 11–15. *Setting a reminder in Google Calendar.*

Obviously, we all want to be on time. With the alarm and reminders options available in Windows Phone 7, we can be sure that a given time (and its associated appointments) will not pass us by!

Chapter 12

Using and Customizing the Calendar

Windows Phone 7 provides a clean and easy way to see your entire list of upcoming appointments. It also provides just the right amount of detail you need, depending on whether you're rushing to an appointment (e.g., where is it?) or setting up a complex reoccurring appointment (e.g., every fourth day of the month). In this chapter, we'll walk through the steps of accessing and customizing the **Calendar** app, as well as adding, editing, and removing appointments.

Accessing Your Calendar and Customizing Its Colors

Getting into the **Calendar** and changing the view is as easy following these simple steps:

1. Turn on your phone and unlock it.

2. Press the **Calendar** live tile. It is one of the few double-column tiles on the **Start** screen, and it shows the date and your next appointment (see Figure 12–1).

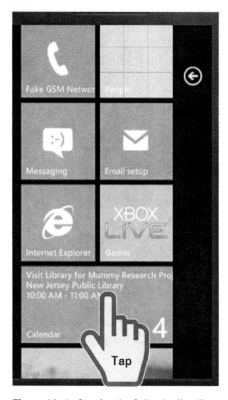

Figure 12–1. *Opening the **Calendar** live tile.*

A screen similar to that shown in Figure 12–2 will appear, showing your appointments for today.

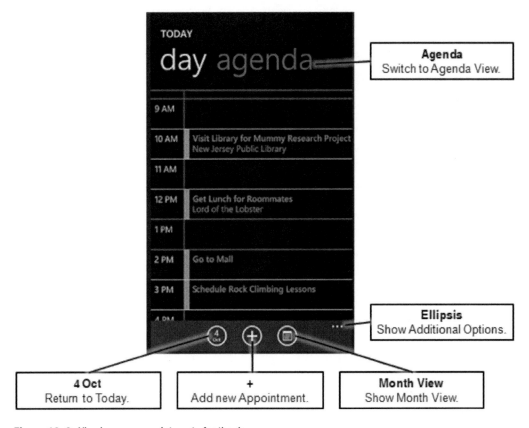

Figure 12–2. *Viewing your appointments for the day.*

3. By default, the **Calendar** displays appointments in a grid format, showing empty spaces throughout the day. If you want to see all of your appointments listed without any space between them (perhaps you have an extremely busy schedule or appointments that overlap, with no space anyway!), tap **Agenda** to switch to **Agenda** view (see Figure 12–3).

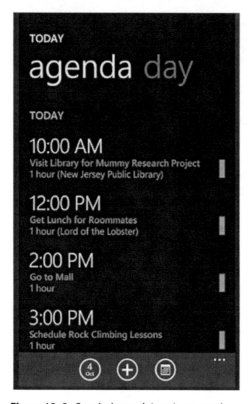

Figure 12–3. *One day's appointments or agenda.*

4. Sometimes you need to see a view of the month (or multiple months ahead), and you want to get a quick idea of how busy you'll be. Tapping the **Month** button switches to this view (see Figure 12–4). You can flick your finger up or down to scroll to future or past months. The days with appointments will show small lines of text to indicate how many appointments you have that day—the more lines, the fuller your schedule is! (Don't ruin your eyes by trying to read the lines, though—they're just meant to show there is an entry, not to list each one!). This view is a great way to scope out your schedule weeks or months ahead, such as when planning trips or vacations. You can also tap a given date to view the schedule for that day. To return to the **Day** or **Agenda** view, hit the **Back** button.

Figure 12–4. *The Month view of your calendar.*

5. If you have multiple accounts set up on your phone, you'll see multiple calendars. You may want to customize the color assigned to each calendar (for example, to separate your calendar from your spouse's or kids' calendars) or turn off calendars entirely. To do this, press the **Ellipsis** key and click **Calendars**.

> **NOTE:** Windows Phone 7 doesn't support showing multiple calendars on the same account. For example, **Google Calendars** allows you to create multiple calendars that can be toggled on and off. However, your Windows Phone 7 device will only show your default calendar.

6. A screen similar to the one shown in Figure 12–5 will appear. For each calendar, you can press the **Off/On** switch to hide or show its entries. You can also tap the **Color** icon to change colors for each calendar, allowing you to customize your view as needed.

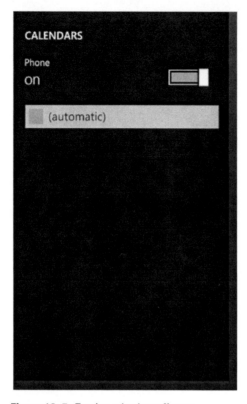

Figure 12–5. *Turning calendars off or on.*

Adding a Calendar Appointment

Adding a calendar appointment is easy to do. You can do so either by filling out the minimum amount of information or by customizing multiple options:

1. Access your **Calendar** by tapping the **Calendar** live tile from the **Start** screen.

2. Tap the **Add** button (see Figure 12–6).

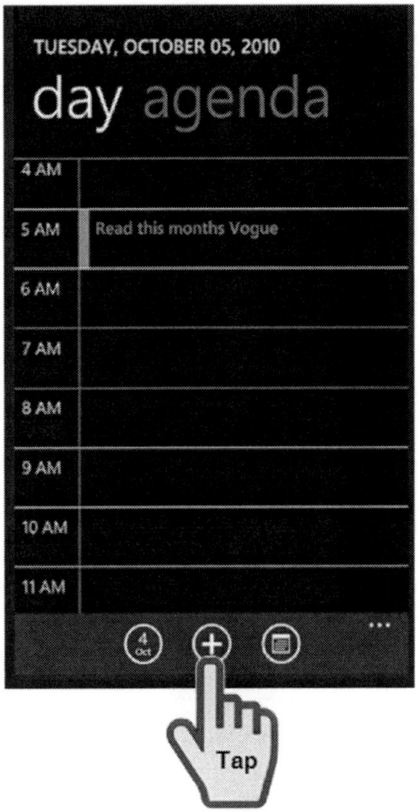

TUESDAY, OCTOBER 05, 2010

day agenda

4 AM	
5 AM	Read this months Vogue
6 AM	
7 AM	
8 AM	
9 AM	
10 AM	
11 AM	

Tap

Figure 12–6. *Adding an appointment.*

3. A screen similar to the one shown in Figure 12–7 will appear. Enter the text description of the appointment in the **Subject** box and the location of the appointment in the **Location** box.

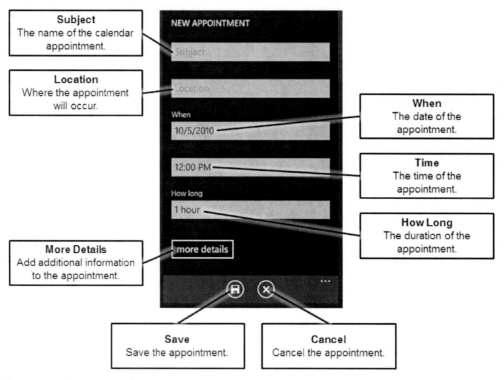

Figure 12–7. *The new appointment screen.*

4. To adjust the date and time, tap the date, and then tap the month, day, or year to adjust. A list of choices will appear at the top and bottom of the element you're changing, and you can scroll through with your finger to the correct month, day, or year (see Figure 12–8).

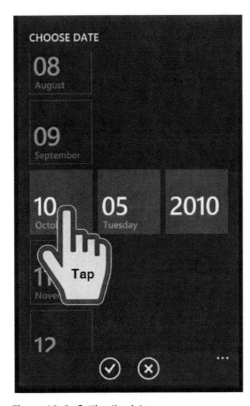

Figure 12–8. *Setting the date.*

5. If you need to add more details, tap the **more details** button. The next section will discuss each of these options.

Understanding and Setting Appointment Details

Windows Phone 7 allows you to set a number of appointment details that work closely with **Microsoft Outlook** on the desktop and, if applicable, your corporation's **Exchange** mail server. Clicking the **more details** button while adding or editing an appointment brings up a number of options (see Figure 12–9):

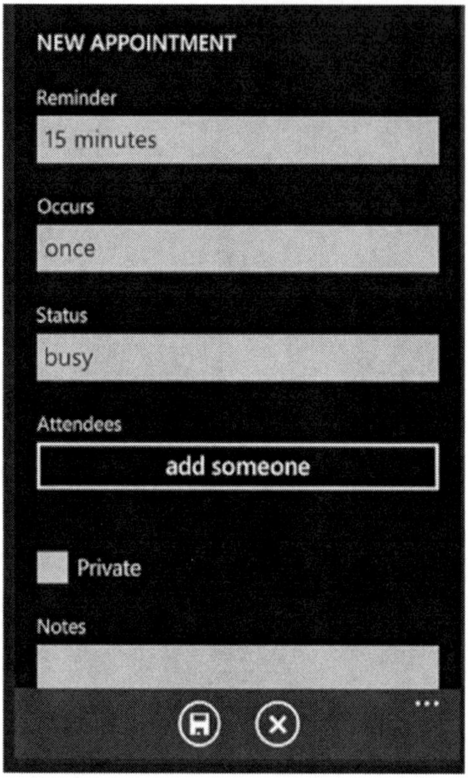

Figure 12–9. *Editing an appointment.*

- **Reminder**—This option allows you to set up a reminder for the appointment. Options range from no reminder (**None**) to a week in advance, with more options closer to the appointment (e.g., 5 minutes or 15 minutes) than farther away (e.g., 18 hours, 1 day, or 1 week). These reminders not only show on your phone, but also show up on your computer if you synchronize your phone and calendar to an **Exchange** server or **Windows Live**.

- **Occurs**—This option, shown in Figure 12–10, can be used for appointments that reoccur at some point in the future. Your **Calendar** will then show each appointment in the upcoming months. You can specify a number of options from your phone; however, to create especially complex calendaring options, you may need to use **Microsoft Outlook** (see Figure 12–11).

OCCURS

once

every day

every weekday

every Tuesday

day 5 of every month

every October 5

Figure 12–10. *Changing recurrence information.*

Appointment Recurrence ☒

Appointment time

Start: 11:00 AM ▼

End: 11:30 AM ▼

Duration: 30 minutes ▼

Recurrence pattern

○ Daily   Recur every 1 week(s) on:

◉ Weekly   ☐ Sunday   ☑ Monday   ☐ Tuesday   ☐ Wednesday

○ Monthly   ☐ Thursday   ☐ Friday   ☐ Saturday

○ Yearly

Range of recurrence

Start: Mon 10/4/2010 ▼   ◉ No end date

                          ○ End after: 10 occurrences

                          ○ End by: Mon 12/6/2010 ▼

[OK]   [Cancel]   [Remove Recurrence]

Figure 12–11. *Setting recurrence in Outlook.*

- **Status**—This option lets you set whether the appointment should be shown as **Busy**, **Free**, **Tentative**, or **Out of the Office** on your calendar. This is useful when your phone is synchronized to a **Microsoft Exchange** server because it allows your colleagues to see whether you are free or busy during a given time period, but without forcing you to show the details of your appointment (e.g., they can see one block of time is "busy" while others are open).

- **Attendees**—Clicking **Attendees** lets you select required and optional attendees to invite to your appointment, provided you already have them in your **People** tile's contact list (see Figure 12–12). Once you save your appointment, appointment requests will be emailed to all of your attendees. This tells them the date and time of the appointment, as well as any pertinent information you've added. They can then click a button to accept, reject, or tentatively accept your appointment request, and you can check the status of these requests using **Microsoft Outlook**.

Figure 12–12. *Specifying attendees.*

■ **Private**—If you share your calendar through a **Microsoft Exchange** server or other shared calendar service, you can check this box to make the details of an appointment visible only to you, not to others who have permission to view your calendar.

■ **Notes**—You can use this section to create any notes you may need to reference about the appointment. In the past, I've filled in this field by simply dropping an email message in **Microsoft Outlook** onto the **Calendar** button. This creates a new appointment, putting the text of the email into the **Notes** box. From here, you can use your phone to read the email before meeting with the person to bring yourself up to speed!

TIP: Adding a person's telephone number in the **Notes** section of an appointment can be a great time saver. Windows Phone 7 will recognize the phone number and allow you to dial it by tapping it. This is perfect for on-the-go situations or even conference calls with nasty long codes you must enter: the number and code go nicely in notes, ready for use!

Editing or Deleting a Calendar Appointment

Editing (changing) or deleting (removing) a calendar appointment should be a fairly simple affair—and it is in Windows Phone 7:

1. Access your calendar by tapping the **Calendar** live tile from the **Start** screen.

2. Tap the appointment you wish to edit (see Figure 12–13); this brings up the **Appointment Details** screen.

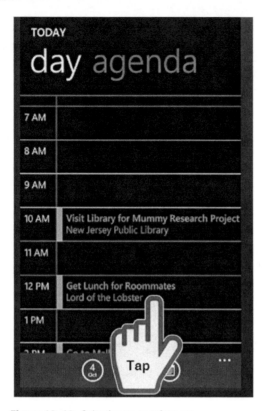

Figure 12–13. *Selecting an appointment.*

3. A screen similar to the one shown in Figure 12–14 will appear. To edit the appointment, tap the **Edit** button. To remove the appointment, tap the **Delete** button.

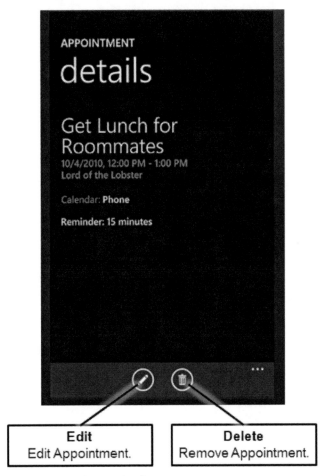

Figure 12-14. *Appointment detail screen.*

As you can see, managing your **Calendar** with Windows Phone 7 is simple and easy. The phone provides information when you need it (by displaying the next appointment right on the **Start** screen's Calendar live tile), and it also allows you to drill down into the appointment's details, even allowing you to invite others to an appointment right from your phone. You can also manage multiple calendars, and customize the appearance of each; this helps you distinguish between your appointments easily!

Chapter 13

Using Text Messaging

Email may rule the land while you sit at your desk, but text messaging is a universal mobile-communication method—all phones have text messages, which means you can use them to communicate with your not-so-tech-savvy friends who still use basic phones. Windows Phone 7 makes it easy to send, receive, and read text messages, as we'll explain in this chapter.

Starting a Text Message

Windows Phone 7 offers two basic ways to send a text message:

Messaging Live Tile—Tap the **Messaging** live tile on your **Start** screen, then tap the **New** button at the bottom of the screen (see Figure 13–1).

Figure 13–1. *Sending a text message from the **Messaging** tile.*

People Live Tile—Tap the **People** live tile on your **Start** screen, then choose the person you wish to text. Tap **text mobile** to start a new message (see Figure 13–2).

Figure 13–2. *Choosing a phone number to send a message to.*

Sending Messages and Pictures

You can do more than send text messages: you can also spice things up by sending pictures. You can send a message to one person, or to multiple people. In this example I'll send the same message to two people, I'll also attach a photo and send it to them as well.

However, I could have simply selected one of them. Windows Phone 7 groups messages into conversations, which means that as I send messages in this conversation, both recipients will get them. If I want to send something to only one of the recipients, I can simply create a new message as previously discussed.In this next example I'll send the same message to multiple people.

1. Start a new text message, as described previously.

2. If you started from the **Messaging** tile, you'll need to add the name of the person you'd like to text. If you started from the **People** tile, it will already be entered (although you can follow this step to add another). To add a recipient, tap the **Add** button in the upper right and choose a contact (see Figure 13–3).

> **NOTE:** If you know the name of the person, you can also tap the **To:** box and type it in directly. Windows Phone 7 will pull a list of possible people as you type and let you select the person's number. If you want to go "old school" and enter the number directly, you can do that, as well!

Figure 13–3. *Selecting contacts to send the message to.*

3. Enter the text you want to send, and tap the **Send** button (see Figure 13–4).

Figure 13–4. *Sending the message.*

4. You can send a photo to both people in the message conversation. To do so, attach a photo, click the **Attach** button, and either choose an existing picture or take a new picture by tapping the **Camera** button at the bottom of the screen (see Figure 13–5).

Figure 13–5. *Taking a new picture to attach.*

5. Once the picture is attached, you can type your message and tap **Send**. If you want to remove the picture, tap the **Remove** button (see Figure 13–6). If you had wanted to, you could also have typed part of the message and then attached the photo (and even typed more text after that)!

Figure 13–6. *Removing a picture.*

Managing Conversations and Text Messaging Settings

Windows Phone 7 keeps track of your on-going text message conversations, grouping your sent texts and responses together so you can easily follow the individual chains of thought. The preceding conversation is shown in Figure 13–7.

Figure 13–7. *The messages list.*

Deleting a Conversation

The night after your epic breakup with your girlfriend is probably not the time you want to see happy conversations with her from three weeks ago! Thankfully, you can delete specific conversations by tapping and holding the conversation, and then choosing Delete from the menu that pops up!

NOTE: You can also delete a conversation from within a conversation—just tap the **Ellipsis** button and choose **delete conversation**—this will take you back to your **Conversations** or **Start** screen.

Text Messaging Settings

There aren't many text messaging settings you can change, but there are two you can change. On the Conversations screen, tap the Ellipsis button and choose Settings. A screen similar to the one shown in Figure 13–8 will appear. From here, you can turn on SMS delivery confirmation. (This tells your cell phone provider's network to send you a text message when your recipient has received your original message; this is helpful in situations where you have limited coverage and you want to be sure a message was received). You can also change the SMS center number; however, you'll want to check with your provider first to ensure you don't change it incorrectly and lose the ability to send or receive text messages. In general, changing the SMS center number without being told to by your cellular provider is a very bad idea!

Figure 13–8. *Messaging settings.*

Text messaging is not as sophisticated as email, but it is an important tool when communicating with others on smartphones or regular cell phones. It can also be used to access services or send verification codes (e.g., in mobile banking). Your Windows Phone 7 device will not only let you send and receive messages, but it will also help you keep them organized. The ability to use pictures to organize conversations (and other files) will also make it more interesting to use!

Chapter 14

Surfing the Web With Internet Explorer

Often one of the primary uses of our desktop and laptop systems is one we shy away from on a phone: viewing webpages. It is true that transitioning from the large, luxurious monitor we may have at our desk to a smaller, handheld device comes with limitations. However, the latest generation of mobile web browsers (such as **Internet Explorer** in Windows Phone 7) makes the experience of browsing something to be enjoyed, not feared!

Starting Internet Explorer and Browsing to a Page

The most basic task is simply to start the browser and head over to a favorite web page. The steps that follow will get you surfing quickly!

> **NOTE:** Some websites have *mobile versions* of their pages. This means that the content you see on a smartphone, such as your Windows Phone 7 device, will look substantially different from what you would see on your desktop computer. In some cases, these mobile pages can be disabled—look for a link toward the bottom of the page that reads "Full Site" or "Exit Mobile Version." In other cases, you'll need to change your preferences to view the full site, something we'll explain how to do later in this chapter.

To get started, turn on your device and unlock it. You should be at the **Start** screen. If not, press the **Windows** key to return to it. Follow these steps to browse the Web.

1. Tap the **Internet Explorer** icon (see Figure 14–1).

Figure 14–1. *Tapping Internet Explorer so you can surf the Web.*

The browser will open, showing a screen similar to the one shown in Figure 14–2. We'll discuss what each option does over the next few pages.

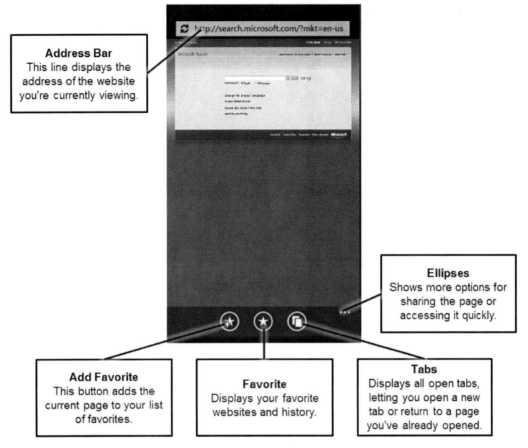

Address Bar
This line displays the address of the website you're currently viewing.

Ellipses
Shows more options for sharing the page or accessing it quickly.

Add Favorite
This button adds the current page to your list of favorites.

Favorite
Displays your favorite websites and history.

Tabs
Displays all open tabs, letting you open a new tab or return to a page you've already opened.

Figure 14–2. *The Internet Explorer navigation buttons.*

2. Tap the **Address Bar** and the on-screen keyboard will appear. Use it to enter a website address. Once you've entered the address, tap the **White Arrow** button in the lower right (see Figure 14–3), and the browser will go to that page.

Figure 14–3. *Navigating to a website.*

3. To zoom in on any portion of the page, double-tap it. Double-tapping again will zoom out. You can also press-and-drag the screen to view portions of the page not shown while zoomed in, as well as pinch-and-stretch any portion of the screen to zoom in or out gradually. Pinching-and-stretching works just as it sounds—you place two fingers (usually your thumb and forefinger) on the screen and slowly move them together (pinch) or apart (stretch) to change the zoom. You may also find it easier to view a page by rotating your device into **Landscape** mode, rather than holding it vertically (**Portrait** mode).

> **TIP:** As you type the address of a website, your Windows Phone 7 device will suggest commonly visited sites to you, allowing you to quickly tap the address of a site to go to it. This list will also show you the addresses of pages you've recently visited, again saving you the time of typing in a complete address!

Using and Managing Your Favorite Sites and History

Your phone will keep a record of your recent site visits, as well as your favorite sites. This is similar to how your desktop browser behaves. The following steps walk you through how to use and manage your favorite sites and history:

1. To view your list of favorite websites, tap the **Favorites** button at the bottom of **Internet Explorer**'s screen (see Figure 14–4).

Figure 14–4. *Accessing favorite sites.*

2. You can tell the browser to go to any of the pages in the **Favorites** list by tapping its name.

3. You can also edit an entry or delete it altogether. Tap and hold the entry until the **Edit** and **Delete** options appear (see Figure 14–5). Pressing the **Edit** button will let you change the name and URL (address) of the entry.

Figure 14–5. *Modifying favorites.*

4. To show your history of recently viewed pages, press the screen and swipe to the left to show the **History** list (see Figure 14–6). Alternatively, you can tap the partial word "history," and the screen will roll over to display your recently viewed pages.

Figure 14–6. *Accessing browser history.*

5.   You can delete your browsing history by tapping the **Delete** button ![delete] (see Figure 14–7). Your phone will ask you to confirm that you want to delete the history. Press **Yes** and you'll be free of those tragic browsing memories (or evidence)!

Figure 14–7. *Deleting history.*

Working With Tabs

Browsing web pages on a computer changed radically when the first browsers to support tabs were introduced. You probably remember using a browser (or perhaps you're still forced to) that doesn't support tabs, spawning several dozen browser windows over the course of a busy work day. Tabs allow you to keep multiple pages open at a time in a single browser instance, which makes switching from page to page a breeze. The following steps walk you through opening multiple tabs and working with them:

1. From **Internet Explorer**'s screen (see Figure 14–2), tap the **Tabs** button.

2. A screen similar to the one shown in Figure 14–8 will appear, showing your current page in the upper left. Tap the **New** button to open a new tab.

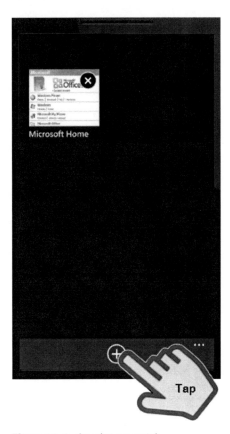

Figure 14–8. *Opening a new tab.*

3. A new tab will open, showing a gray background and asking you to enter the web address of the site you'd like to open (see Figure 14–9). You'll notice the **Tabs** button now shows the number of open tabs: two! To browse to a new site, you can either enter the address or select an entry from your **Favorites** or **History**. Let's head over to my personal blog, so we can see how it looks on my smartphone!

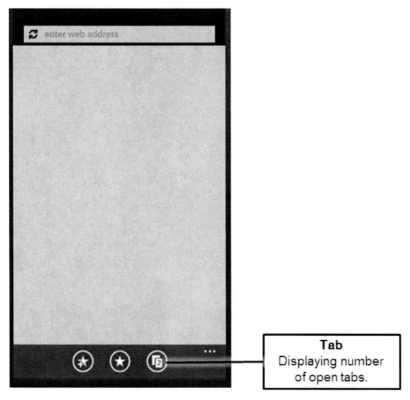

Figure 14–9 *Accessing open tabs.*

4. Now that we've seen my rather boring blog, we decide we probably don't want to keep that tab open! To close a tab, tap the **Tab** button to bring up the **Open tabs** screen and tap the **Close** button ❌ on the upper right of the tab (see Figure 14–10).

Figure 14–10. *Closing an open tab.*

Exploring, Sharing, and Pinning Pages

While browsing a page, you can access different options to work with the page you are currently viewing. To get to these options, press the **Ellipsis** button, as shown in Figure 14–2. Doing so will bring up the following list of options (see Figure 14–11):

Figure 14–11. *Internet Explorer menu options.*

The **forward** option will be available if you recently used the **Back** button to return to a previous page. It will take you forward to the page you were previously on.

The **find on page** option will let you search for text on the page you're currently viewing. This is a great tool when you're looking for a specific piece of information!

The **pin to start** option will let you take your most used pages and put them straight on your **Start** screen. This is perfect for pages you use frequently, such as traffic or weather information, train schedules, or news websites!

The **settings** option lets you configure **Internet Explorer** to behave in certain ways. We'll discuss the available choices in the **settings** option in more detail in the next section.

Configuring Internet Explorer Settings

Internet Explorer can be configured to behave in certain ways. While you probably will not need to change the default settings (Figure 14–2), the following list describes each choice and why you may want to change it:

Figure 14–12. *Internet Explorer Settings.*

> **Allow cookies on my phone**—Despite the tasty sounding nature of this option, cookies to a web browser are seldom as exciting as they are to humans. A cookie is a small piece of information, usually in text form, that a website saves on your computer. This may be your username for the website or your preferences. As mentioned, previously, many mobile versions of websites will store your viewing preferences in a cookie. Other websites won't work well (or even at all) without cookies. However, if you're concerned that a website may be storing information on your phone that you'd rather it didn't (or you notice a website acting strangely on second and subsequent visits), you may want to disable cookies by unchecking this box.

Let Bing suggest sites as I type—Bing is Microsoft's search engine (or, as Microsoft brands it, a decision engine—whatever that is). You may recall I mentioned earlier that, when typing in a web address, **Internet Explorer** may suggest addresses similar to the one you're typing. Normally, this saves you time because it lets you tap directly on the address and browse to the site more quickly; however if you don't like Bing's suggestions, go ahead and uncheck this box.

Website Preference—When **Internet Explorer** browses to a page, it identifies itself as either a mobile browser or a desktop browser. Selecting **Mobile version** tells **Internet Explorer** to identify itself as a smartphone, while selecting **Desktop Version** tells **Internet Explorer** to identify itself as a normal desktop web browser. The site may respond differently depending on this setting. For example, it might show a smaller or optimized version of the site if **Mobile version** is selected, but show a complex version of the site (that may take more time to load) if **Desktop version** is selected. In some cases, you may want to force **Internet Explorer** to identify itself as its desktop version; however, in most cases, **Mobile Version** is probably the best choice.

delete history—We discussed deleting your browsing history previously when we talked about using and managing your list of favorite websites and your browsing history. This button does the same thing as the one we discussed before, but it provides a bit more detail on what exactly it deletes or clears. One thing it does not delete is your list of favorite websites—those will remain after deleting your history!

Privacy Statement—Many people are concerned with how the information they put into a phone will be used, or how a search engine may use the information it collects on their search patterns. This link will take you to Microsoft's official privacy statement, giving you more information on these matters.

As you can see, **Internet Explorer** on Windows Phone 7 is a powerful web browser that's also easy to use, which makes finding and navigating to your favorite sites quick and easy!

Chapter 15

Taking Pictures and Putting Them Online

Windows Phone 7 includes a number of features designed to make taking and working with pictures easy. This chapter talks about the **Pictures** live tile and the built-in camera on your device. All Windows Phone 7 devices are required to have at least a five megapixel (MP) camera, a resolution sufficient to replace your point-and-shoot camera on your daily adventures. Couple the high-resolution camera with the fact that it's possible to take and post a photo to SkyDrive or Facebook in less than 10 seconds, and your Windows Phone 7 device is ready to capture all of the action quickly and easily!

Exploring the Pictures Live Tile

The **Pictures** live tile acts as a central hub for all of your photos, whether you've taken them with your phone or uploaded them to Facebook or SkyDrive. It also shows you photos your friends have taken and uploaded! The following steps walk you through how to access your pictures:

1. Turn on and unlock your phone.

2. Tap the **Pictures** live tile (see Figure 15–1).

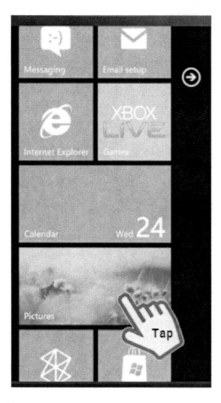

Figure 15–1. *Opening the Pictures Live Tile.*

3. The screen that appears will display either the **pictures** menu (see Figure 15–2) or your photos. Take your finger and swipe from right to left to move through the different pane and view your photos. One of these panes (see in Figure 15–3) is the **what's new** section. If you've hooked up a SkyDrive or Facebook account (see Chapter 3), photos your friends have uploaded to those two services will be displayed here. Once you've swiped through all of the panes, return to the main **pictures** menu (see Figure 15–2).

Figure 15–2. *The **Pictures** hub.*

Figure 15–3. *The **what's new** pane.*

4. Tap the **all** option in the main **pictures** menu. A screen similar to the one shown in Figure 15–4 appears.

Figure 15–4. *Browsing pictures.*

5. From this screen, you can either tap an album (e.g., the **7** album shown in the Figure 15–4); or you can swipe your finger from right to left see photos in your **favorites** group or to see your photos sorted by date. I've tapped the **7** album, which you can see in Figure 15–5.

Figure 15–5. *Browsing the 7 photo album.*

6. Pressing and holding any photo brings up the context menu shown in Figure 15–6. This menu allows you to take the following actions on a photo: **delete**, **share...**, or **add to favorites** (through messaging or email). Adding a photo as a favorite makes it appear in the **favorites** group mentioned in the previous step.

Figure 15–6. *Picture options.*

7. Simply tapping one of the photos shown in Figure 15–5 will enlarge it to fill your screen (see Figure 15–7). Rotating your phone into **Landscape** mode may help the photo fill the screen better, if it was originally taken in **Landscape** mode!

Figure 15–7. *Viewing a photo.*

8. Pressing the **Ellipsis** button allows you to work with the photo in a few ways (see Figure 15–8). You can add it to the **favorites** group, delete it, upload it to SkyDrive (if you've set up a Windows Live account), share it, or use it as wallpaper for your **Lock** screen.

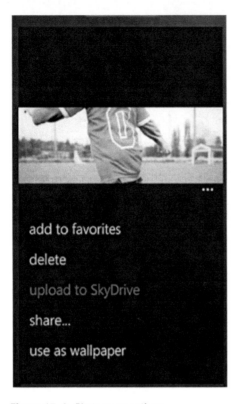

Figure 15–8. *Photo menu options.*

Taking a Picture

Taking a picture with Windows Phone 7 is really easy! Follow these simple steps to do so:

1. Press and hold the **Camera** button (it's usually on the side of your device) for two to three seconds. Your phone will turn on and display the **Viewfinder** screen (see Figure 15–9).

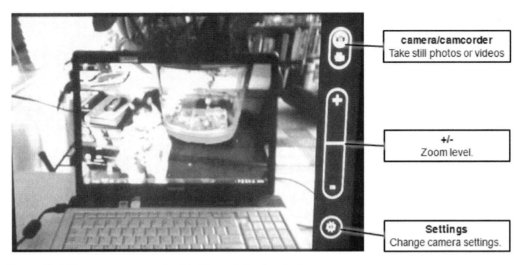

Figure 15–9. *The camera screen, about to take a photo of my laptop.*

2. Tapping the **Gear** icon will bring up the **Camera** settings (see Figure 15–10). These settings let you change the **Scenes** (predetermined settings for picture taking), **Effects**, **Resolution**, **Metering Mode**, and **Flicker Adjustment**. You can also toggle the flash between **always on**, **always off**, and **auto on**.

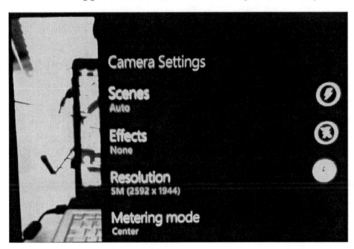

Figure 15–10. *Camera options.*

3. To take a picture, press the **Camera** button halfway down to focus, then press the button the rest of the way to take the picture.

4. To view previous pictures, swipe your finger from left to right to show previous pictures in your camera roll.

5. You can also view all of your previous photos by pressing the **Start** button and browsing the **Pictures** live tile, as discussed previously in this chapter.

Sharing Photos With Others

Windows Phone 7 allows you to share photos in a three different ways. The following list covers all the ways to share photos on your device, including the pros and cons of each method:

- **Manually share photos via email or messaging**: As you saw in the preceding section, the **Pictures** live tile makes it easy to bring up a photo and tap the **share** option. Doing so will attach the photo to an email or message. You can then address the email or message and send it on its way. The pro of this approach is that it allows you to share the photo with specific people, and you always know when a photo has been shared. The con, however, is that you must remember to share each photo, and this could become tedious when sharing more than a couple of photos.

> **TIP:** In Chapter 23, "Connecting to the Zune Software", we'll discuss setting up your phone to connect with the **Zune** desktop software. When you connect your phone to the Zune service, it will automatically download your photos to your computer. This approach provides another way to share your photos that doesn't involve your phone! Simply use a tool to upload the photos to a website, attach them to an email, or embed them in documents!

- **Private Upload to SkyDrive**: The first time you take a photo after adding a Windows Live account, you'll be asked whether you want to upload your photos automatically and whether you'd like photos you upload set to public or private. Setting photos to upload to SkyDrive, marked so that only you can see them, is another easy way to share them. To do this, simply go to your computer, navigate to www.skydrive.com, log in, and download the photo. You can then email it or upload it to another site. The only downside to this approach: The extra steps mean that it takes longer after you take a photo for your friends to see it.

- **Public Upload to SkyDrive or Facebook**: If you're a diehard social butterfly, this might be the best option for you. It will simply upload all of your photos to your SkyDrive or Facebook publicly, so that everyone can see them as soon as you take them. This is definitely the easiest way to share your photos, but it also raises a bit of a privacy concern. You need to make sure you don't take any photos you wouldn't want the whole world to see!

Setting Picture and Camera Options

You can configure the camera and photos on your Windows Phone 7 in a number of ways. Follow these steps to access and change the **picture + camera** settings:

1. Turn on and unlock your phone.

2. Press the **Arrow** icon in the upper right to access the **application list**, then press **settings** (see Figure 15–11).

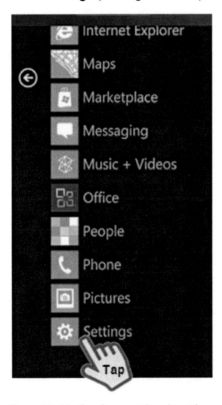

Figure 15–11. *Opening your phone's settings.*

3. Press and slide to the left to access **applications** settings, then touch **pictures + camera** (see Figure 15–12).

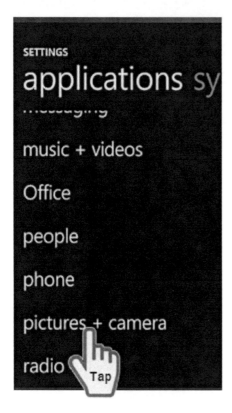

Figure 15–12. *Opening **pictures + camera** settings.*

The **pictures + camera** settings will appear (see Figure 15–13). The remaining steps each deal with a section of these settings.

Figure 15–13. *The pictures + camera settings.*

4. The first setting asks whether you would like the **Camera** button to wake the phone. One of the best features of Windows Phone 7 is the speed with which you can take a photo. Even if the phone is locked, pressing and holding down the **Camera** button will wake the phone and allow you to snap a picture. However, if you do not want this functionality to work (e.g., perhaps you don't want others snapping pictures with your locked phone!), then you can disable it by setting the slider to **Off**.

5. The next setting deals with storing location data (GPS) in photos you take. This can be helpful when later matching photos to a location (e.g., when taking a trip, it can help you remember where you were when you snapped the picture). However, if you do not want the photos *geotagged* (as the feature is known), then you can disable it. As an added benefit, disabling the feature will also conserve power and extend your battery life!

6. If you have added a Windows Live account to the phone, you can set the next slider to **On** to have it automatically upload all photos taken to Windows Live SkyDrive.

7. If you would prefer photos uploaded to Windows Live SkyDrive not be tagged with your GPS location (i.e., so that others can't tell where a given photo was taken), set this slider to **Off**. Note that this does not affect the geotagging discussed in the previous step; photos taken and stored on the camera will still be geotagged.

8. The last section deals with quick upload accounts, which currently include Facebook and SkyDrive. Your phone can be set to automatically upload photos to either Facebook or SkyDrive if you've added those accounts to your phone. This setting lets you configure that option or disable auto upload altogether.

9. The last link takes you to the Windows Phone Privacy statement, assuming you would like to read it.

Your Windows Phone 7 device can act as a fairly feature-complete camera, great news if you're one of those people who carries a camera in your bag or purse to capture all of life's special moments. Even if you're not an aspiring or chronic photographer, your Windows Phone 7 device will allow you to snap a photo and share it whenever and wherever you need to!

Chapter 16

Using Windows Live Services

Your Windows Phone 7 device can do pretty much everything you need out-of-the-box. However, Microsoft has built into your phone a number of connections to free services that Microsoft also owns. It's what marketing folks call a *value-added relationship*; however, for common users like you and me, it translates to a bunch of cool things that you can take advantage of. In previous chapters, we discussed setting up a Windows Live ID; now we'll discuss a few services that you can use both on your phone and on your PC that help you get the most out of your new Windows Phone 7 device. In this chapter, we'll discuss the Windows Live SkyDrive, Windows Live Profiles, and Office Online services.

Windows Live SkyDrive: the Storage

Creating new documents, spreadsheets, notes, pictures, and more on your phone can be a double-edged sword. Sure, it's great to have that content on your phone, but how do you actually access it when you're at your desktop? Starting a list or taking a snapshot might be fine on the go, but it's worthless if you can't finish it later or save it to your picture collection.

Fortunately, your Windows Live Account includes access to SkyDrive, a free service you can access at `http://www.skydrive.com.` SkyDrive is a free service from Microsoft that provides 25 GB of storage space. You can upload files (Such as documents, spreadsheets, or photos) to your SkyDrive account, and can access these files anywhere you have an Internet connection, from your home PC to your laptop, and even on your Windows Phone 7 device!

If you haven't done anything with your SkyDrive account, visiting the website will show you something like what you see in Figure 16–1. For the purposes of this example, we'll assume you haven't added any files or synchronized anything yet. However, we'll also assume you would like to keep a few files on SkyDrive, so you can access them from other computers or your phone. The steps that follow will walk you through creating a new folder, uploading files, and working with them on your phone:

Figure 16–1. *A Windows Live SkyDrive account.*

1. On your computer, go to http://SkyDrive.live.com and log in with your Windows Live ID and password.

2. Click **Add Files** in the top toolbar (see Figure 16–2).

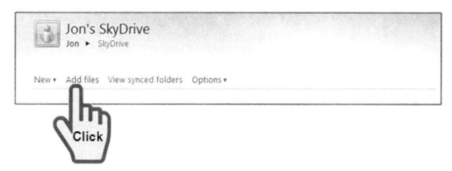

Figure 16–2. *Adding files to your SkyDrive account.*

3. A screen will appear that lists the folders you've created in SkyDrive. To create a new folder, click **New Folder** and enter a name for the folder on the next screen (see Figure 16–3).

Figure 16–3. *Creating a folder in SkyDrive.*

4. A screen similar to Figure 16–4 will appear. You can drag-and-drop files from your desktop into the box, or you can click **select more documents** to bring up a **File Open** box. From here, you can navigate to your files and select the ones you want to upload.

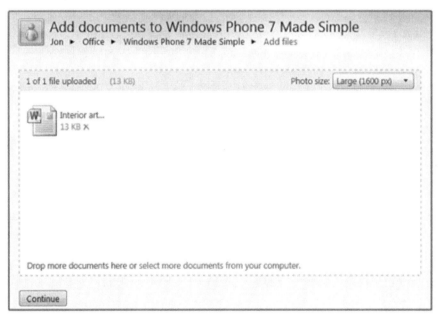

Figure 16–4. *Adding files to your newly created folder.*

5. When done, click **Continue**. A screen similar to the one shown in Figure 16–5 will appear. From this screen, you can do a number of things. For example, clicking a file lets you work with it in your browser or with other programs on your computer. You can also share the entire folder with other people or download the whole folder as a ZIP file.

Figure 16–5. *The upload has been successful!*

6. If you want to store files that can be synchronized to your computer, you can upload them to a special area, and then download the **Windows Live Mesh** client. You can find out more about this ability by going to http://devices.live.com. For now, we'll continue by discussing how to access a document on SkyDrive from your phone.

7. Turn on and unlock your phone.

8. Tap **Internet Explorer** (see Figure 16–6).

Figure 16–6. *Opening Internet Explorer.*

9. Tap the address bar and type http://skydrive.live.com.

10. On the **Windows Live Sign In** screen, type your Windows Live ID and password (see Figure 16–7).

Figure 16–7. *Signing into Windows Live.*

    11. Once logged in, tap the file you wish to open or the folder you wish to access (see Figure 16–8).

Figure 16–8. *Viewing your uploaded SkyDrive documents on your phone.*

TIP: You can bookmark your favorite SkyDrive folders or documents and even pin them to your **Start** screen. To make the best **Start** screen icon, zoom into the portion of the screen you want to see on the **Start** screen and select **pin to start** from the menu (tap the **Ellipsis** button to see this option).

Connecting With the World: Windows Live Profiles

If you plan on using your SkyDrive account, you may also want to share files with others. In the preceding figures, you can see that my own Windows Live account wasn't particularly interesting to look at. For example, my profile information was empty, and my friends could see only a silhouette photo and my name, which isn't very personable if I want to share pictures through Windows Live or other services such as Facebook. The following steps outline how to set up a Windows Live Profile and connect it to other services you might use:

1. On your computer, go to http://profile.live.com and log in with your Windows Live ID and password.

2. You should see a screen similar to the shown in Figure 16–9. This screen displays a completely blank profile that is ready for customization!

Figure 16–9. *A Windows Live Profile.*

3. As you can see from the previous figure, you must first decide how much information you want to share by default. Initially, your profile is set to **Limited**, which means that friends you approve within Windows Live can see your shared pictures and profile activity. You can also change this to **Public**, which will let everyone view your shared pictures and activity; or **Private**, which will restrict your information, so only you can see it. I'm going to set my own account to **Limited**. Press **Save** to continue.

4. After you set your privacy settings, Windows Live shows you how complete your profile is. This is a quick way to see how much personalizing you have left to do. You will also be asked whether you'd like to upload a photo, which you can do by clicking **Add a photo** (see Figure 16–10).

Figure 16–10. *Adding a photo to your profile.*

5. After you upload your photo (Perhaps of a Pirate Pumpkin, like mine), Windows Live asks whether you'd like to set your birthday, so that everyone can wish you a great day (while covertly reminding you how old you're getting!). Choose whichever option you prefer; as for myself, I'll submit to the public ridicule and add my birthday to my profile. Click **Save** to continue (see Figure 16–11).

Figure 16–11. *Updating your personal information.*

6. Next, Windows Live asks a few more questions. Do you want to set your location? (I'll enter "Earth" and press **Save**.) Do you want to set a mobile number, so your friends can contact you easily? (My profile is **Limited**, so that sounds like a good idea to me—this way, friends who have a Windows Phone 7 device will automatically get my phone number in their address books!)

7. Finally, your profile is complete (see Figure 16–12 for my completed profile). Now you can connect your Windows Live account to other services if you choose, including Facebook, YouTube, Linked In, and MySpace. Linking your accounts together means that you can post a note in Windows Live, and your friends on those other services will see it, without requiring that you post this information repeatedly.

Figure 16–12. *My profile is now complete, and I can connect it to other services.*

8. The last step is to post a quick note, which you can type (see Figure 16–13) and then post. You can see posts your write on the **Me** live tile on the **Start** screen; you can update your status from there, as well!

Figure 16–13. *Posting an update or note.*

Using Office Online

Sometimes you can't work from a computer that has **Microsoft Office** installed. Perhaps you don't even own **Office** at home and only use it at work or school. Thankfully, Microsoft has released the Office Online service, a suite of web applications that let you work with your **Office** files on the go. The following steps explain how to edit a file and viewing those edits on your phone:

1. On your PC, go to http://office.live.com and log in with your Windows Live ID and password.

2. A screen similar to the one shown in Figure 16–14 will appear. This demo will walk you through how to create a new **Word** document, so click **Word** under **Create a new online document** on the right.

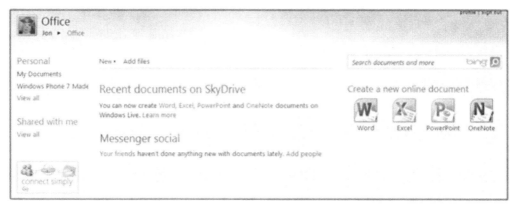

Figure 16–14. *Microsoft Office Online.*

3. Windows Live asks you what to name your new file; enter a name and press **Save** (see Figure 16–15).

Figure 16–15. *Creating a new **Word** document.*

4. An empty **Word** document appears (see Figure 16–16). Note that this document displays the **Ribbon** toolbar common to all **Microsoft Office** applications. Begin by making a list of fun things you might do with your cat and then use commands on the **Ribbon** to format the list to your liking.

Figure 16–16. *The **Word Online** toolbar.*

5. Once you finish adding and formatting the text, click the **Save** icon in the upper left (see Figure 16–17).

Figure 16–17. *Saving your new **Word** file.*

6. Now imagine you're at home. You've shared a tuna sandwich with the cat, and you're at a loss for what to do next. So you take out your Windows Phone 7 device and consult the list you made previously.

7. Follow Steps 7—11 in the "Windows Live SkyDrive: the Storage" section to access your SkyDrive account from your phone.

8. Tap the document you created earlier (see Figure 16–8). A preview window opens, showing the contents of the file (see Figure 16–18).

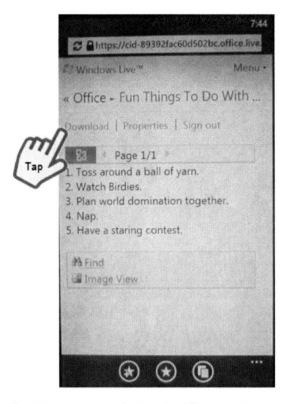

Figure 16–18. *Downloading your* ***Word*** *file to your phone.*

9. To open the file in **Mobile Word** for editing, tap the Download link (see Figure 16–18).

10. Tap the link to open the file in **Mobile Word** (see Figure 16–19).

Figure 16–19. *Opening a **Word** file on your phone.*

11. Edit the file in **Mobile Word** (see Figure 16–20). You can also refer to Chapter 18: "Using Microsoft Office Mobile Word" for information on using **Word Mobile**).

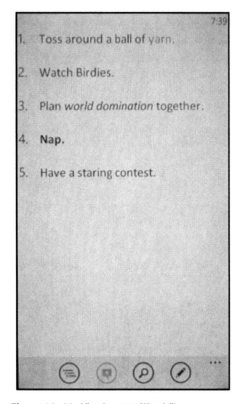

Figure 16–20. *Viewing your **Word** file.*

As you can see, Microsoft has a number of interesting online tools available in the Windows Live suite of services, including SkyDrive, Profiles, and Office Online. The integration of these services with Windows Phone 7 means that you can work with files on your computer and easily access them on your Windows Phone device. All indications are that this integration will only get stronger over time!

Chapter 17

Using Microsoft OneNote Mobile

For many years, whenever I had some notes I needed to take or keep (such as in my undergraduate years in college), I used a full-fledged word-processor (e.g., **Microsoft Word**). This worked for my needs, but **Word** wasn't really designed for taking either on-the-fly notes or the more formal notes required for a class or meeting. Responding to this need, Microsoft introduced **OneNote** in 2003. This application was created specifically for taking notes (in text, pictures, and voice or audio recording). Your Windows Phone 7 device ships with a special version of **OneNote** that includes the special ability to synchronize your notes to your Windows Live SkyDrive account, letting you take your notes on the go and view them on your computer later (or vice versa)!

Viewing and Creating Notes

We'll get started by walking through how to open **OneNote** and then view a few notes that are already on your phone:

1. Turn on and unlock your phone.

2. Tap the **Arrow** icon in the upper right of the screen to access the **applications list**. Next, move the list up and tap **Office** (see Figure 17–1).

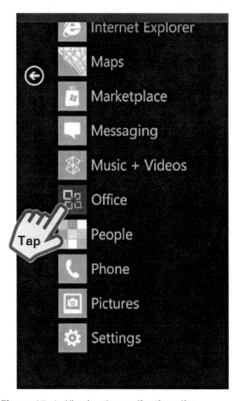

Figure 17–1. *Viewing the applications list.*

3. A screen similar to the one shown in Figure 17–2 will load on the **OneNote** section, conveniently enough. The interface is pretty simple. You can add new notes by pressing the **new note** button, view all of your notes in a list format by pressing the **all** button, or see the most recently accessed notes in blocks below the two buttons.

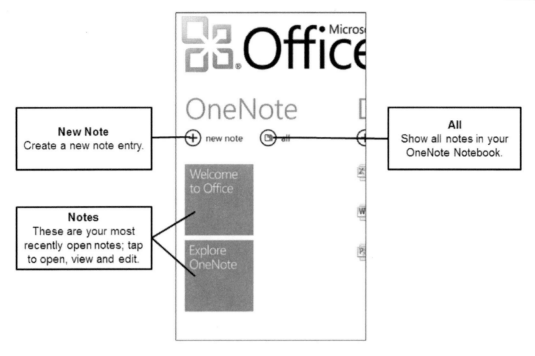

Figure 17–2. *The OneNote screen in the Office Hub.*

4. To view a note, simply tap the box with the name of the note you wish to view. Or, if the note isn't on the first page, press the **all** button and select the note. For example, tapping the *Welcome to Office* note displays the screen shown in Figure 17–3.

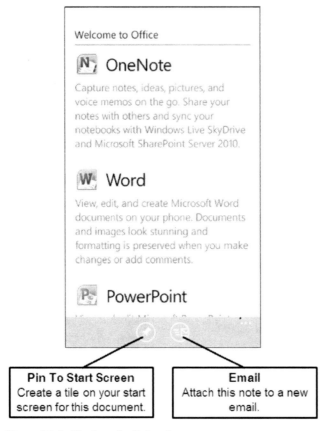

Figure 17–3. *Viewing a OneNote note.*

5.   If you like, you can edit the note by tapping the text. Doing so will make the
keyboard appear. At this point, you can select or edit text (see Figure 17–4).

Figure 17-4. *Editing a OneNote note.*

6. To save your changes, simply press the **Back** button on your device. Your changes will be automatically saved, and you'll return to the main **OneNote** menu.

Getting Fancy: Lists, Pictures, and Formatting

Next, let's create a quick note. Along the way, we'll look at how to create a list of your favorite musical groups, add pictures, and apply formatting:

1. Follow Steps 1–3 under the earlier "Viewing and Creating Notes" section to get to the screen shown in Figure 17–2.

2. Tap the **new note** button, and a blank note will load (see Figure 17–5).

Figure 17–5. *A blank note.*

3. Pressing the **Ellipsis** button brings up many different options for taking notes. You can add lists, pictures, and audio (which you'll learn how to do in the steps that follow). You can also **undo** your last change, **redo** a change you just undid, create a **bulleted list**, **increase** or **decrease** your **indent** level, and change the **format** (see Figure 17–6).

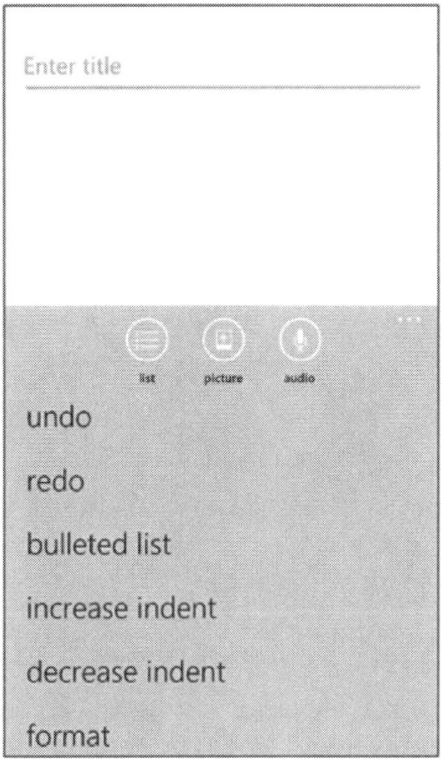

Figure 17–6. *Menu options.*

4. Tap the top of the note where it reads **Enter title** and give the note a new title: **Best Musical Acts** (see Figure 17–7).

Figure 17–7. *Creating a list.*

5. The next step is to create a list. However, when you tap the **list** button, you're given a numbered list (see Figure 17–8). Let's assume you don't want to prioritize the list by numbering. Tap the **Ellipsis** button and choose **bulleted list**; this changes the list to a bulleted one.

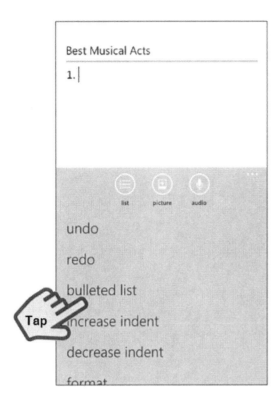

Figure 17–8. *Changing to a bulletted list.*

6. With the bullets in place, you're ready to enter your own completely subjective list of best musical acts. In my own example, I first tapped out four bullet points, and then decided to speak the name of an artist I wasn't exactly sure how to spell. This way, I could look up the spelling later, when I was at my computer and my extensive music library. Begin by typing in a couple of your own favorite acts, then tap the **audio** button to add an audio note to the list, as well (see Figure 17–9).

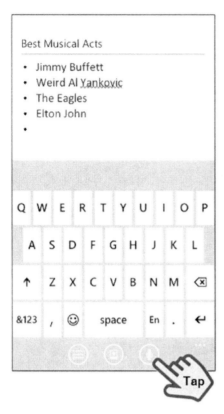

Figure 17-9. *Adding an audio note.*

7. While the phone records your audio, you'll see a screen similar to the one shown in Figure 17-10. When you're done, tap **stop**.

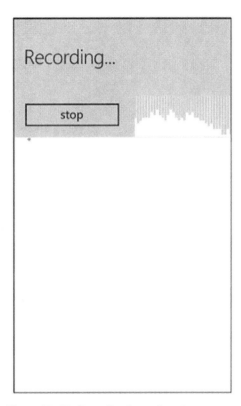

Figure 17–10. *Recording the audio note.*

8. As shown in Figure 17–11, a small **Page** icon appears with a speaker. Tapping this icon will play your voice note. Your voice is now included in the note, but now you decide you'd also like to include a picture. Tap the **Picture** button. This brings up the standard picture chooser, which lets you grab a photo from your camera roll on the device or other pictures you have access to. Once selected, the picture appears in the note.

> **TIP**: **OneNote** will process your photos and add optical character recognition (OCR) data. This means that reasonably legible handwriting will be searchable—letting you do cool things such as snap a picture of a whiteboard and later find text written on it when searching your phone.

Figure 17–11. *Adding a picture.*

9.   At this point, you're done editing, so you can simply press the **Back** button. This displays your note (see Figure 17–12 for my version of this note). Hitting **Back** once more returns you to the main **OneNote** menu.

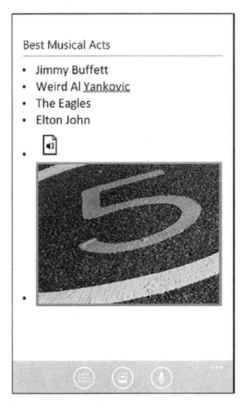

Figure 17–12. *The inserted picture.*

10. But wait! While you're at this menu (see Figure 17–13), you realize you'd like to make one of the entries bold. Tap **Best Musical Acts** to bring the note back up.

Figure 17–13. *The OneNote screen in the Office Hub.*

11. Tap within the note to bring up the editing keyboard, and then use your finger to select the first act by pressing and dragging your finger over the text. You want to change the format, so once the text is selected, press the **Ellipsis** key and choose **format** (see Figure 17–14 for my version of this list).

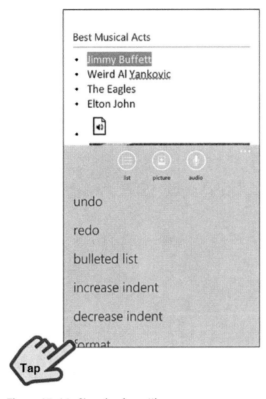

Figure 17–14. *Changing formatting.*

12. The **Format options** screen appears (see Figure 17–15). Tap the **bold** button.

Figure 17–15. *Formatting options.*

13. Now when you return to the note, you can verify the text is in bold-face type (see Figure 17–16). When you're satisfied with your edits, you can hit the **Back** button and go about your day!

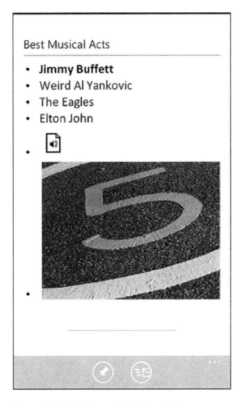

Figure 17–16. *The updated formatting.*

Pinning, Sharing, and Searching Notes

You can work with **OneNote** notes quickly, share them with others, and search all of your notes with ease. Follow these steps to leverage each of these features:

1. Follow Steps 1 – 3 under the earlier "Viewing and Creating Notes" section to get to the screen shown in Figure 17–2.

2. As shown in Figure 17–17, there is another list on my device that is a "work in progress" called **Worst Musical Acts**. Let's assume that you want to **Pin** this note to your **Start** screen, so that you can easily add new items to it as you're moving around town. Tap and hold the **Worst Musical Acts** tile until the pop-up menu appears. Next, tap the **pin to start** option.

Figure 17–17. *Pinning a note to start.*

3. The item would now appear on your **Start** screen (see Figure 17–18). Now let's assume you want to send your friend Ye a copy of the **Worst Musical Acts** list. Ye finds a lot of music enjoyable, so you want to make sure he steers clear of these acts, lest he begin hating music in general!

Figure 17–18. *Pinned note on the **start** screen.*

4. Tapping the note from the **Start** screen brings it up. From here, you can tap the
    Email button at the bottom of the screen (see Figure 17–19).

Worst Musical Acts

- South American Screaming
Monkey Quartet
- Nailz on the Chalkboardz (extreme
heavy metal)
- Angry Lemur Boys
- Maroon 5

Tap

Figure 17–19. *Emailing a note.*

5. If you have multiple email accounts set up, the next screen will ask you to select
    one. After doing so, a new email will appear with your note attached. Simply
    select a recipient for the email (see Chapter 4: "Using Email" for more information)
    and press **Send**.

6. Now assume a few months have elapsed, and you've made many more additions
    to the **Worst Musical Acts** list. You'll want to reference this list, just to make sure
    you didn't exclude any horrendous bands. To search your notes, follow Steps 1 –
    3 to get to the screen shown in Figure 17–2. Next, tap the **all** button.

7. Press the **search** button on your phone, and a box will appear above your list of
    notes (see Figure 17–20). Typing part of a word (or in this case a single letter) will
    begin to filter down the list to titles that match the search criteria. From here, you
    can quickly find the exact note you're looking for.

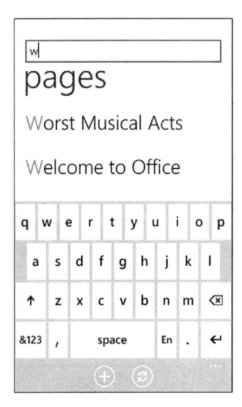

Figure 17–20. *Searching for a note.*

Synchronizing Notes With SkyDrive

One of the best uses for **OneNote** on your device is to take notes on your phone and then view or work with them on your computer (or vice versa). Follow these steps to set up your phone to synchronize with Windows Live SkyDrive quickly and easily:

1. You'll need to add at least one Windows Live account to your phone (see Chapter 3: "Setting up Accounts" for more information on adding accounts) before you can use this feature.

2. Once you have a Windows Live account set up on your phone, follow Steps 1 – 3 under the earlier "Viewing and Creating Notes" section to get to the screen shown in Figure 17–2.

3. From the main **OneNote** screen, press the **all** button. A screen similar to the one shown in Figure 17–21 will appear.

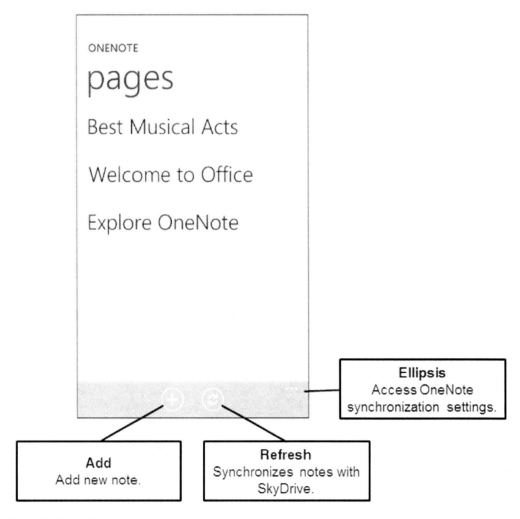

Figure 17–21. *OneNote pages options.*

4. Press the **Refresh** button. If this is your first time synchronizing with a SkyDrive account, a message similar to the one shown in Figure 17–22 will appear, asking if you'd like to enable synchronization.

Figure 17–22. *SkyDrive sync message.*

5. If you do not have a Windows Live account set up, you'll receive a message similar to the one shown in Figure 17–23. This message informs you that you'll need to sign into a Windows Live account to continue.

Figure 17–23. *Windows Live ID Required message.*

6. Once the synchronization process finishes, you can customize the sync settings by pressing the **Ellipsis** button on the **All notes** page (see Figure 17–21) and choosing **settings**. The **OneNote** settings will appear (see Figure 17–24). You can choose to automatically have your notebooks updated on a regular basis (the default is **On**, as shown in Figure 17–24), or you can disable automatic synchronization. If you disable automatic synchronization, you'll need to manually press the **Refresh** button within any note you want to save or download the changes from. This **Refresh** button will appear on the **Main** menu bar, next to the **Pin** and **Email** buttons (see Figure 17–3).

Figure 17–24. *OneNote Sync options.*

7. Once your notebooks are synchronized, you can view them online by visiting
    `http://skydrive.com` and clicking **My Documents**. You'll see a list of documents
    appear similar to the ones shown in Figure 17–25. The notebook that you will
    work with both on your device and on the web is named **Personal (web)**.

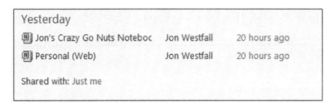

Figure 17–25. *Listing of notebooks on SkyDrive.*

8. Hovering your mouse over the **Personal (web)** notebook will give you multiple options. You can choose **edit in browser**, and **OneNote Web App** (see Figure 17–26) will open, letting you make edits through your browser. You can also choose **open in OneNote** if you have Microsoft **OneNote** installed on your computer. This will open **OneNote** on your computer and load up your shared notebook, letting you enter text through the program on your PC and have it synchronize with your phone! Any edits you make through either method will be downloaded by your phone the next time it synchronizes or you press the **Refresh** button.

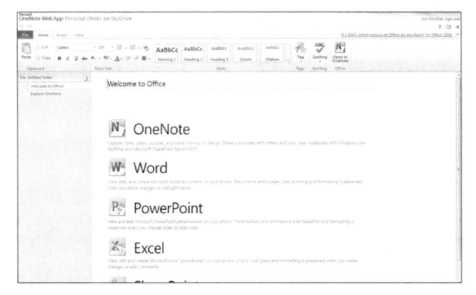

Figure 17–26. *Editing a notebook in SkyDrive.*

NOTE: To open a new notebook on your phone other than **Personal (web)**, you'll need to use **Internet Explorer** on your phone to navigate to http://live.office.com, log in with your Windows Live ID, and then tap the notebook you wish to open.

In situations where a full word processor might not be appropriate, you can now use the powers of **Microsoft OneNote Mobile** to view, create, keep, and edit notes of all sizes. For the most flexibility, you can also use **OneNote** on the desktop to edit these notebooks!

Chapter 18

Using Microsoft Office Word Mobile

Chances are, like most people, you use **Microsoft Office** at work. Even if you don't use **Office**, you are probably required to open **Office**-formatted documents (e.g., files ending in .doc, .docx, .xls, or .xlsx) from time to time. Your Windows Phone 7 device contains a version of **Word** specifically designed to let you view and edit documents straight from your phone. This chapter will explain how to use **Microsoft Office Word Mobile** to create new **Word**-based files and edit existing files.

Starting Word and Creating a New File

We'll begin by firing up **Word Mobile** and creating a new file. Follow these steps to do so:

1. Turn on your phone and unlock it. Depending on your phone model, you may find the **Microsoft Office Mobile** tile on the **Start** screen, or you may have to press the **Arrow** icon in the upper right to see the **applications list**. Find the entry for **Office** and tap it (see Figure 18–1).

Figure 18–1. *Viewing the applications list.*

2.   A screen similar to the one shown in Figure 18–2 will appear, showing **Microsoft Office Mobile OneNote**. We'll discuss **OneNote** in a later chapter. For now, simply press the screen, hold, and swipe to your left to bring up the **Documents** screen.

Figure 18–2. *Navigating the Office Hub.*

3. Once the **Documents** screen displays, tap **new document** (see Figure 18–3) and choose **Word document**.

Figure 18–3. *Creating a new document.*

4. A blank document will open; once it does, you'll be able to enter text into this document (see Figure 18–4).

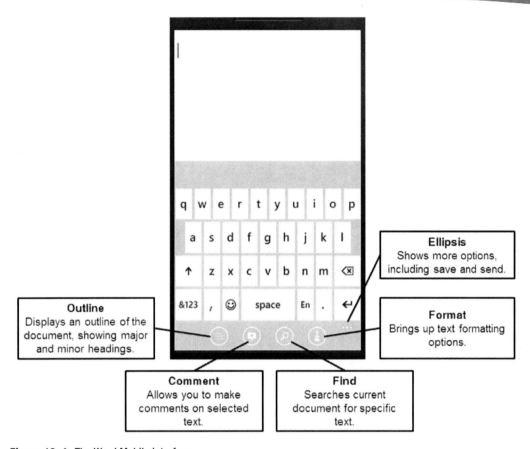

Figure 18–4. *The Word Mobile interface.*

Editing a Document

The editing features of Windows Phone 7's **Word Mobile** software allow you to not only view documents, but also to make changes, add comments, and change formatting. The steps that follow will walk you through creating a sample document and making changes to it:

1. Follow the steps outlined in the earlier "Starting Word and Creating a New File" section to create a new file.

2. Enter some sample text into the document.

3. Pick a word that you'd like to change the formatting for. Tap your finger twice on the word to highlight it. Or, you can tap at the beginning of a portion of text, then drag your finger across the text to highlight multiple words (see Figure 18–5 for an example of what a highlighted word looks like).

> **TIP:** Tapping and holding the text will bring up an **Ibeam** cursor, allowing you to place your cursor exactly where you'd like it when entering new text or correcting mistakes.

Figure 18–5. *Changing formatting on a word.*

4. As you can see from Figure 18–5, **Word** will suggest alternatives for you if you accidentally misspell a word. In this case, the letters in "awesome" are apparently too close to the letters in "sardine" and "assails." Neither was the word I wanted, so I didn't tap them.

5. Tap the **Formatting** button (see Figure 18–4) to bring up **Mobile Word**'s formatting options (see Figure 18–6). Choose one or more of the available formatting options to apply to the text, as desired. For example, you might choose to make the text bold and two sizes larger. After each formatting change, you'll be taken back to the document, and you will need to re-press the **Formatting** button to apply additional formatting.

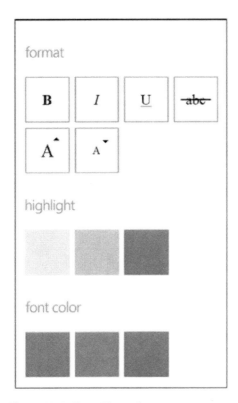

Figure 18–6. *Formatting options.*

6. Once your text is formatted, you're ready to add a comment to the document. You add a comment in **Mobile Word** much as you add a comment in the desktop version of **Microsoft Word**. To do so, highlight the section you want to add a comment to (in this case, the whole sentence) and press the **Comment** button (see Figure 18–4). Next, enter a comment about the text (see Figure 18–7 for an example I created). To finish editing the comment, tap anywhere outside the highlighted text.

Figure 18–7. *Adding a comment.*

7. As Figure 18–8 illustrates, the text you add a comment to displays with a blue
    highlight. The lower-left part of this highlight includes a tiny point (representing a
    speech bubble) to indicate that it's a comment. Tapping it will show the comment.

Figure 18–8. *Tapping on a comment.*

8. Be sure to experiment with your document; this will give you a feel for **Mobile Word**'s features and how they work. When you're finished, press the **Back** button on your phone, and **Mobile Word** will ask whether you want to save the document.

Opening a Document

You can open a previously saved document by following these simple steps:

1. Turn on and unlock your device.

2. Open the **Office** live tile. You may need to press the **Arrow** icon in the upper right of your **Start** screen and scroll down to **Office** first.

3. Press, hold, and slide to the left to bring up the **Documents** view (see Figure 18–2).

4. Tap the name of the document you wish to edit (see Figure 18–9), and it will open for reading.

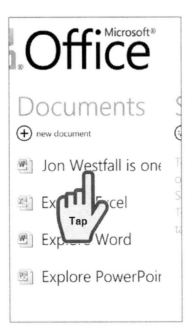

Figure 18–9. *Opening a document.*

5. To edit or make changes, tap the **Edit** button (see Figure 18–10).

Figure 18–10. *Editing a document.*

Word Menu Options

In Word Mobile, pressing the Ellipsis button will bring up various options, as shown in Figure 18–11. What follows is a description of what each option does:

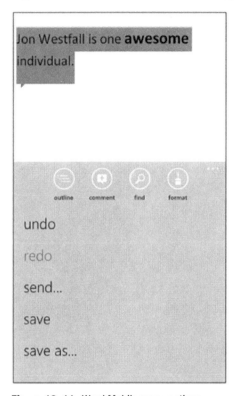

Figure 18–11. *Word Mobile menu options.*

- **Undo**—While editing, you may sometimes make a mistake, apply formatting you don't want to keep, or make a comment you'd like to remove. Pressing **Undo** will roll back your previous change, removing it and letting you re-edit the section more to your liking.

- **Redo**—If you **Undo** a change and then decide you actually liked it better, you can press **Redo** to restore the change.

- **Send…**—This option lets you send your work via email to your colleagues or friends. Pressing it prompts you to save your document (if you have not already) and then attaches it to an email that you can then address. You must have set up at least one email account on your device for this feature to work.

- **Save**—This option saves the current document. If you haven't saved the document previously, you will be prompted to provide a file name for it.

- **Save as...** — This option allows you to save the document under a new name. This is best for creating a new version of the document after you've made substantial changes. It allows you to keep the old version of your document (under the old name), while also saving your changes (under a new name). You could also use this as a sort of backup mechanism—saving versions of your file as you edit in case something happens and you would like to revert to an earlier draft.

Chapter 19

Using Microsoft Office Excel Mobile

Since its introduction, **Microsoft Excel** has grown in both ability and complexity. Today it sports a feature-rich environment for creating everything from to-do lists to multi-sheet ledgers to thousand-line data summaries. On your Windows Phone 7 device, you can use **Microsoft Office Excel Mobile** to view, create, and edit files that you can then share with colleagues or open on your desktop computer.

Starting Excel Mobile and Creating a New File

Let's begin by firing up **Excel Mobile** and creating a new file. Follow these steps to do so:

1. Turn on your phone and unlock it.

2. Depending on your phone model, you may find **Microsoft Office Mobile** on the **Start** screen, or you may have to press the **Arrow** icon in the upper right to show the **applications list**. Find the entry for **Office** and tap it (see Figure 19–1).

Figure 19–1. *Opening the* **Microsoft Office Mobile** *suite.*

3. A screen similar to that shown in Figure 19–2 will appear, showing **Microsoft Office Mobile OneNote**. Press the screen, hold, and swipe to your left to bring up the **Documents** screen.

Figure 19–2. *Navigating to the Documents pane.*

4. Once the **Documents** screen displays, tap **new document** (see Figure 19–3) and choose **Excel Workbook**.

Figure 19–3. *The Documents pane.*

5.   At this point, you will see a blank spreadsheet that displays rows and columns (see Figure 19–4).

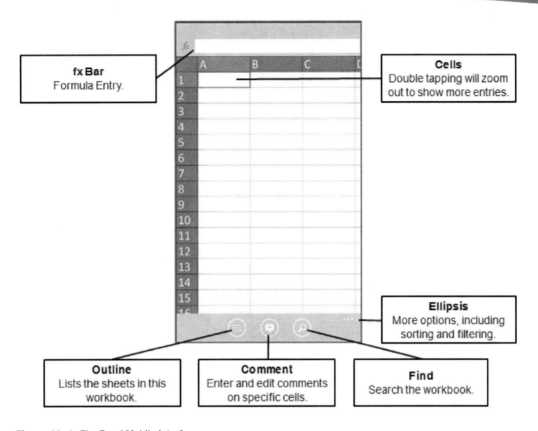

Figure 19–4. *The Excel Mobile interface.*

Editing a Spreadsheet: Entering Data

You probably won't be creating any thousand-line spreadsheets on your phone, but you can use **Excel Mobile** to create useful and dynamic spreadsheets wherever you are. In the steps that follow, you'll learn how to enter data into cells, use formulas, and format a cell:

1. Follow the steps outlined in the earlier "Starting Excel and Creating a New File" section to create a new file.

2. Next, you want to make a list of items. You can pick anything you like to categorize, of course. But for the purposes of this example, we'll assume you have a number of sport coats and lapel pins, and you want to know how many unique pairs you can make with them. Begin by listing the items in **Excel Mobile** (see Figure 19–5).

Figure 19–5. *Editing a cell in Excel Mobile.*

3. To calculate the number of combinations, you need to know how many items are in each list. You can use the **Sum** function to accomplish this. Begin by tapping cell A8 and entering this formula: =counta(a2:a7).

4. In cell B8, you enter a similar formula: =counta(b2:b7) (see Figure 19–6).

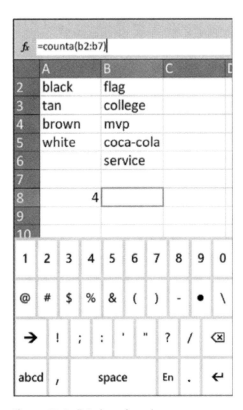

Figure 19–6. *Entering a formula.*

5. Now you just need to calculate the number of pairs. Because you can pair each coat with each pin, you can simply multiply the number of coats by the number of pins. This is an easy calculation that you can put in cell C8. Next, put the word "combinations" in C9, so you know what you are calculating!

6. Finally, it might be helpful to format cell C8 so that it stands out better. Tap that cell, tap the **Ellipsis** button, and then choose **format cell.** Click the **Bold** button to apply bold-face styling to the selected cell (see Figure 19–7). At this point, you have a bolded total, but you could use the same method to format other cells.

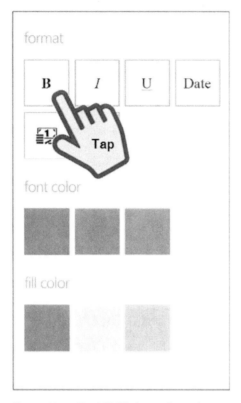

Figure 19–7. *Excel Mobile formatting options..*

Viewing Options

Sometimes you need to find a particular piece of information in a spreadsheet. Sometimes you might need to find just one cell, in which case you could use the **Find** button (see Figure 19–4). Other times, however, you might need to see multiple pieces of data in an easy-to-understand format, where the information is filtered and sorted to your liking. The following example walks you through how to filter and sort data.

Assume that you have loaded an **Excel** spreadsheet that displays the names of children in a class and the scores they recently earned on the final exam (see Figure 19–8). You can manipulate this data in several ways:

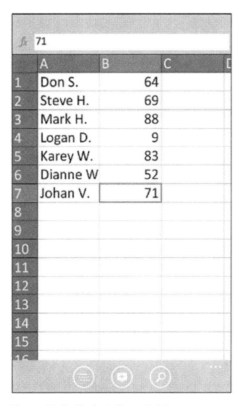

Figure 19–8. *Manipulating cell data.*

- **Sorting**—None of these students performed extremely well on the final. Nonetheless, you might want to sort the spreadsheet, so you can see who performed best at a glance. To do this, tap the **Ellipsis** button and choose **sort...** In the box that appears, sort by ColumnB in descending order. Pressing the **More Options** button at this juncture will let you choose secondary sort options (e.g., sorting students with the same score by name) and allow you to exclude the header row (which you don't have in this case, so there's no need to exclude it here!). After you perform the sort, you're ready to review the results. Figure 19–9 shows both the sorting options and the resulting sorted rows.

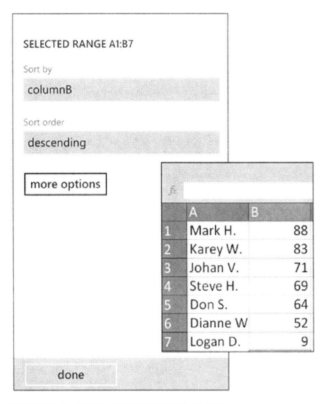

Figure 19–9. *Sorting and the results of the sort.*

- **Filtering**—Assume that this class requires a score of 70 or higher to pass. Thus, you need to filter out anyone who got anything less. Tap the **Ellipsis** button and choose **Apply Filter.** The screen now changes to show small drop-down **Arrow** icons on the first cell in each column (see Figure 19–10). You can tap those **Arrow** icons to see the sorting options. **Excel Mobile** will let you filter discrete values, such as top 10, bottom 10, or all. Unfortunately, this version doesn't let you create a filter on an arbitrary number. Thus, if you need such a filter, you must create it in the desktop version of **Excel**. To make the filter's drop-down **Arrow** icons go away, tap the **Ellipsis** button again and choose **remove filter**.

Figure 19–10. *Applying a filter.*

- **Hiding Columns/Rows**—Perhaps you don't want to see the names of each student. In that case, you can easily hide the entire column by double-tapping the column header (A) and then pressing and holding your finger on the screen to show the column options (see Figure 19–11). From here, you can tap **Hide** to hide the column or use one of the other options described in Figure 19–11.

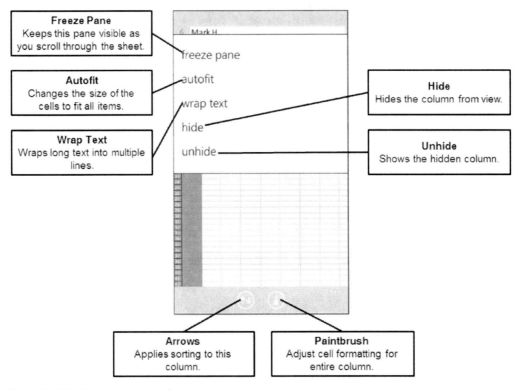

Figure 19–11. *Row and column options.*

- **Formatting Entire Rows/Columns**—Selecting an entire column or row by double-tapping the header (as in the preceding example), also displays the options to sort the row and change the formatting for all of the selected cells (see Figure 19–11).

Similarities to Word Mobile

1. Many of the options available in **Word Mobile** are also present in **Excel Mobile**. What follows is a quick summary of the options common to both applications. Please see the previous chapter for specific information on each feature. Unless otherwise specified, you can access each of the following options using the **Ellipsis** button from within **Excel Mobile** (see Figure 19–12):

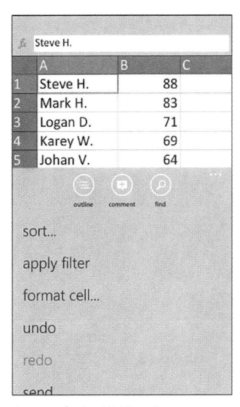

Figure 19–12. *Excel Mobile options.*

- **Commenting**—Pressing this option lets you enter comments for each cell, similar to how you can associate comments with words or sentences in **Word Mobile**. These comments will then be visible to people who view the workbook. You press the **Comment** button to enter your comments (see Figure 19–4).

- **Undo**—Pressing this option rolls back your most recent change to the spreadsheet.

- **Redo**—Pressing this option cancels your previous **Undo**, restoring your change.

- **Send...**—Pressing this option sends your work via email to your colleagues or friends.

- **Save**—Pressing this option saves the current document.

- **Save as...**—Pressing this option allows you to save the document under a new name.

Chapter 20

Using Microsoft PowerPoint Mobile

A common practice before a meeting in my place of employment (and possibly yours) is to circulate prospective **PowerPoint** slides for comments. This means a bevy of emails fly around with slides attached, and comments are requested within a few hours, if possible. It can really be a pain to fulfill such a request if you're on the train, at home, or away from your computer! Fortunately, Microsoft has included a special mobile version of **PowerPoint** with Windows Phone 7 called **Microsoft Office PowerPoint Mobile**. This program lets you view and edit **PowerPoint** slide shows with ease!

Viewing a PowerPoint Document

To get started, we'll walk through how to open a **PowerPoint** slide show. You can do this in one of two ways with the current version of Windows Phone. First, you can open a **PowerPoint** document from a **Sharepoint** server (you'll learn more about **Sharepoint** in the next chapter). Second, you can open a **PowerPoint** document attached to an email by following these steps:

1. If the **PowerPoint** document you want to view hasn't already been sent to you through email, attach it to an email and send it to yourself, so that it appears in your inbox.

2. Turn on and unlock your phone.

3. Open the inbox that contains the email with the appropriate **PowerPoint** document attached, and then open that email message. You'll see something similar to the image shown in Figure 20–1 (see Chapter 4: "Using Email" for more information on opening emails).

Figure 20–1. *Opening a PowerPoint show attached to an email.*

4. Tap the **PowerPoint** document attached to the email. This will tell your phone to download the document. Once the download completes, tap once more to open the document.

5. The slide show will open (see Figure 20–2).

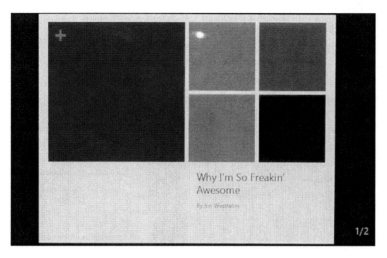

Figure 20–2. *The PowerPoint show explaining why I am so Awesome.*

6.   To move to the next slide or trigger the next animation, press the screen and slide to the left (see Figure 20–3). To move back a slide, press the screen and slide to the right.

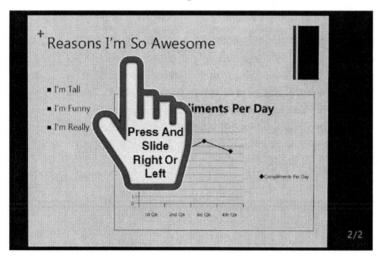

Figure 20–3. *Advancing slides by pressing and sliding.*

Editing a Slide Show

We've got a slide show open; next, we'll walk through editing the slides. Remember that, while Windows Phone 7 allows you to edit text easily on a slide, you will need to perform more complex edits such as layout or image editing on your computer. Still, sometimes all you need is to perform a quick text edit! Follow these steps to edit a **PowerPoint** slide show:

1. Follow the steps in the earlier "Viewing a PowerPoint Document" section to open a slide show.

2. Tap to the right of a slide, and the menu buttons will appear (see Figure 20–4).

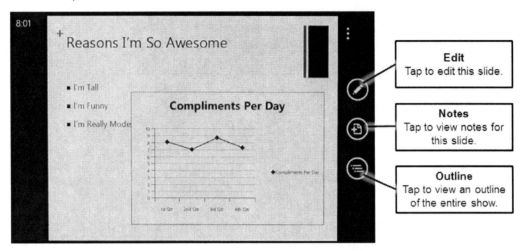

Figure 20–4. *PowerPoint navigation buttons.*

3. Pressing the **Ellipsis** button brings up four more options (see Figure 20–5). **Custom show** is active if your slide show has any custom shows saved in it (you make these using the desktop version of **PowerPoint**). **Send...** lets you send the current **PowerPoint** presentation through email. **Save** is active if you've made any changes to this presentation; choose this option if you wish to save any changes to the **PowerPoint** document to your device. **Save as...** lets you save changes to this document under a new name on your phone.

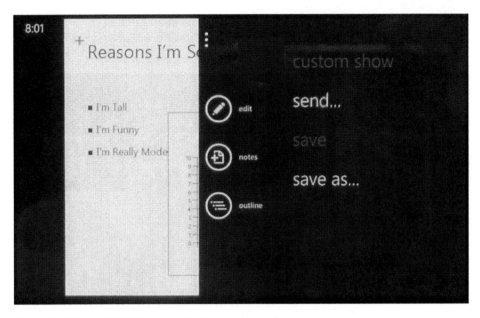

Figure 20–5. *PowerPoint full menu options.*

NOTE: You can save slide shows to your phone; however, to allow others to access them, you must either send them via email or upload them to a **SharePoint** server.

4. You're now ready to edit this document. Tap the **edit** button (see Figure 20–4), so that you can make a few changes. Doing this brings up the editing buttons (see Figure 20–6).

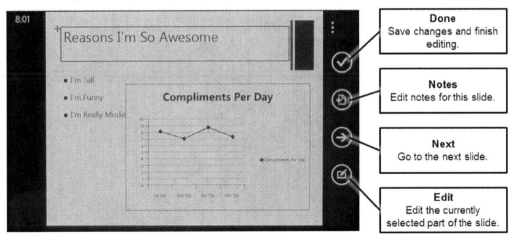

Figure 20–6. *The navigation buttons available while editing a slide.*

5. Pressing the **Ellipsis** button lets you either **move** the slide to another position in the deck or **hide** it so that it won't be shown during a regular presentation (see Figure 20–7).

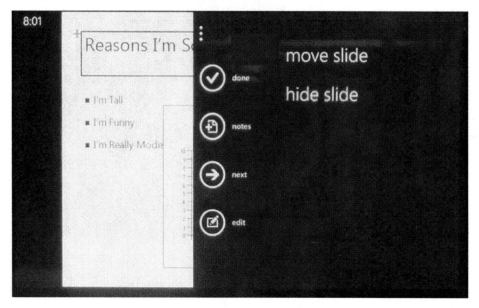

Figure 20–7. *Edit mode menu options.*

6. Editing any single element of the slide is easy. Simply tap the desired element (e.g., the title or a bulleted list) and then tap the **edit** button (see Figure 20–6). A screen similar to the one shown in Figure 20–8 will appear, letting you edit the text. In my example, I added the word "totally" to the slide title for heightened dramatic effect. Choose your own title to edit and make a change to it. Once done, press the **Checkmark** icon to finish the edits.

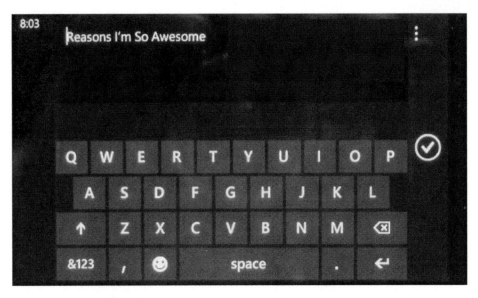

Figure 20–8. *Editing slide text.*

7. Once you finish editing a slide, you can see the updated title in the slide (see Figure 20–9 for my example).

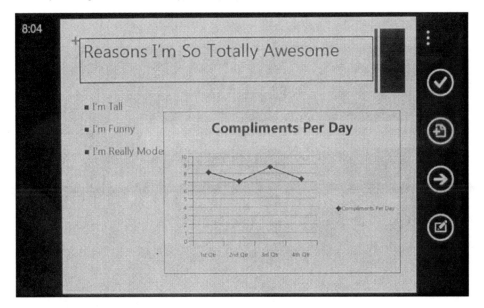

Figure 20–9. *The edited slide.*

8. To finish editing, press the **Back** button. If you've made changes, a box similar to the one shown in Figure 20–10 will appear, asking whether you'd like to your save changes.

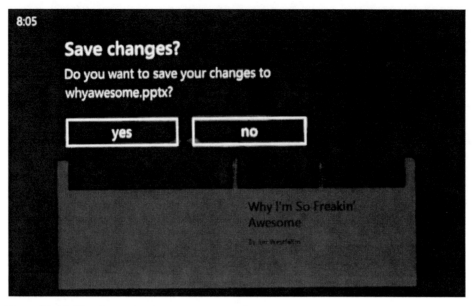

Figure 20-10. *The phone prompts you to save your changes.*

9. If you choose to save changes, a box similar to the one shown in Figure 20–11 will appear, asking for a name to save this presentation as. Naming this document will help you find it on your phone later.

Figure 20-11. *Entering a file name.*

10. If you haven't saved an **Office** document on your phone before, a box similar to the one shown in Figure 20–12 will appear. This box asks you to enter your username. If you're collaborating with colleagues through **Sharepoint**, you may want to use your first and last name. Otherwise, your first name will probably be sufficient.

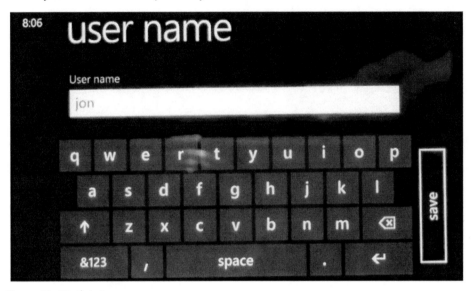

Figure 20–12. *Entering your user name.*

Opening a Saved Slide Show

Now that you've got a slide show saved on your Windows Phone 7 device, it's useful to know how to open it again. Follow these steps to do so:

1. Turn on and unlock your device.

2. Press the **Arrow** icon in the upper right of the screen, then scroll down and tap **Office** (see Figure 20–13).

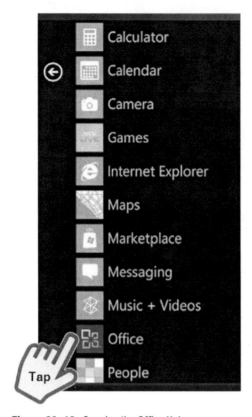

Figure 20–13. *Opening the Office Hub.*

    3.   Press and swipe your finger from right to left to move from the **OneNote** screen to the **Documents** screen (see Figure 20–14).

Figure 20–14. *Navigating to saved documents.*

4. On the **Documents** screen, you can find your saved **PowerPoint** document alongside other saved **Office** documents (see Figure 20–15).

Figure 20–15. *The list of documents on the phone.*

5. Tapping the document will open it, while pressing and holding the
    document for a moment will bring up the menu shown in Figure 20–16.
    This menu lets you **send** the document via email, **delete** the document
    from your device, or view the document's properties. These properties
    display the document's name and file size.

Figure 20–16. *Document editing options.*

PowerPoint is a versatile and fun tool to use. And with Windows Phone 7, you're never far from your **PowerPoint** documents. Not only can you view such documents on your phone, but you can also edit them, save them, and send them to others!

Chapter 21

Connecting to SharePoint

Microsoft **SharePoint** is quickly becoming a staple of many an office worker's life. A system designed to let you share, collaborate, and get work done more easily, **SharePoint** seems like a logical addition to any mobile device. However, only a Windows Phone 7 device thus far lives up to the promise of **SharePoint** on a smartphone. In this chapter, we'll discuss how to connect to your company's **SharePoint** server, allowing you to access work files wherever you may be.

> **NOTE:** Windows Phone 7 requires that your company be running the latest version of **SharePoint Server** (**Microsoft SharePoint 2010**), as well as a **Microsoft Forefront Unified Access Gateway** (**UAG**) server. This ensures that your phone connects securely to the **SharePoint** server. If your company uses an older version of **SharePoint**, or does not have a UAG server, you can still browse the **SharePoint** server in **Internet Explorer** on your phone; however, you cannot connect to it using the **Office Hub**. We'll discuss how to connect to a **SharePoint** server using both of these methods in this chapter.

Connecting to a Microsoft SharePoint 2010 Server

If your company is running **SharePoint Server 2010** and **Forefront Unified Access Gateway** (**UAG**), your Windows Phone can connect directly to the server and browse files. Follow these steps to get started:

1. Turn on and unlock your phone.

2. Tap the **Arrow** icon in the upper right to access the **applications list**, then tap **Office** (see Figure 21–1).

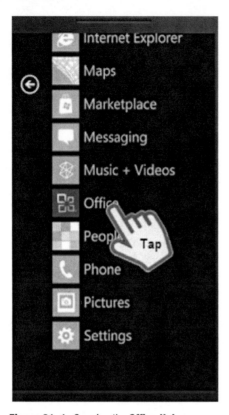

Figure 21–1. *Opening the* **Office Hub**.

3. When the **Office Hub** opens, press and slide your fingers from right to left, switching panes until you see the **SharePoint** pane (see Figure 21–2).

Figure 21–2. *The **SharePoint** pane.*

4.   Tap the **open URL** button.

5.   Enter the address to your **SharePoint** server and press the **Arrow** icon in the lower right of the keyboard to navigate to it (see Figure 21–3).

Figure 21–3. *Opening a **SharePoint** URL.*

6. At this point, your phone will attempt to connect to the **SharePoint**
    server (see Figure 21–4). If all goes well, you will successfully connect. If
    you have trouble, see the "Troubleshooting SharePoint Connections"
    section later in this chapter for some tips on how to fix the problem.

Figure 21–4. *Connecting to the **SharePoint** site.*

7. Your phone will prompt you for your **SharePoint** username, password, and domain (see Figure 21–5). Enter these and press **done**.

Figure 21–5. *Entering your **SharePoint** credentials.*

8. Once you log in, your phone will display the different pages of the
    SharePoint site. In Figure 21–6, you can see that we're on the **Sales
    SharePoint** site for this company, and we can navigate to
    Announcements, **Links**, **Shared Documents**, and more.

Figure 21–6. *Browsing the **SharePoint** site.*

9. Assume that you've tapped the **Shared Documents** link and find that
    there is an **Excel** document on the server you can view (see Figure 21–7).
    Tapping that document will open it in **Mobile Excel**.

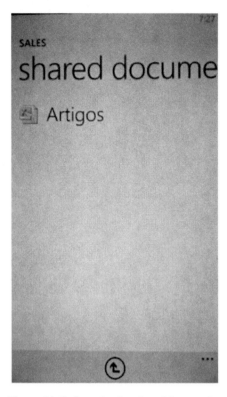

Figure 21–7. *Browsing the shared documents.*

10. Pressing and holding on a document for a few moments brings up more options, as shown in Figure 21–8. These options include the ability to download the file (but not open it), as well as the ability to tell your phone to always keep a copy of this file offline (refreshing it whenever you connect to **SharePoint**). You can also send a link to the file, view its properties, or delete the copy of the file on your phone.

Figure 21–8. *Document options.*

11. On any **SharePoint** screen, you can tap the **Ellipsis** button for more options (see Figure 21–9). These options include the ability to refresh the current view (so you can see any changes that have been made), bookmark the link, and open the site in your browser.

Figure 21–9. *SharePoint menu options.*

12. You may recall that the **Office Hub** has a pane to the right of the **SharePoint** pane, as shown in Figure 21–2. This is where bookmarks from within **SharePoint** servers will appear. If you tap **bookmark this link** (see Figure 21–9), a bookmark will be created, as shown in Figure 21–10.

Figure 21–10. *Bookmarked **SharePoint** locations.*

You've now connected to a **SharePoint** site, which means you can browse and open its files, bookmark different locations, and more!

Connecting to an Earlier Version of Microsoft SharePoint

One great thing about technology is that it's always changing. This is also a problem for those of us who have to maintain it. If your company hasn't had the time, ability, or resources to upgrade to **SharePoint 2010**, you'll need to access your **SharePoint** server through a browser. Follow these steps to do so:

1. Turn on and unlock your phone.

2. Tap **Internet Explorer** to launch the browser (see Figure 21–11).

Figure 21–11. Opening Internet Explorer.

3.   Enter the address of your **SharePoint** server in the address bar.

> **NOTE:** Your company's **SharePoint** server must be accessible to either the Web or the wireless network your phone is connected to before you can access it on your phone.

4.   Your phone will prompt you to enter your **SharePoint** username, password, and domain (see Figure 21–12).

Figure 21–12. *Entering your **SharePoint** site credentials.*

5. After you enter this information, your phone will open the **SharePoint** site (see Figure 21–13); the site should look similar to what you see when accessing the site on your computer. You can now navigate the site as you would any other site in **Internet Explorer**; for example, you can even tap files to open them in **Word** or **Excel!**

Figure 21–13. *Browsing the **SharePoint** site for Dr. Weird's Lab Group.*

Troubleshooting SharePoint Connections

Sometimes things go wrong when connecting to **SharePoint**. Some of these things are fixable on your end, while others will require you to contact your company's system administrator for help in resolving the problem. This section will describe some of the more common errors you may encounter, as well as how to fix them.

Resolving the "Can't Open" Error

Sometimes you get an error indicating that **SharePoint** can't open or doesn't support the site you're trying to open. This error occurs when trying to connect to a **SharePoint** server, and it will look something like the error shown in Figure 21–14.

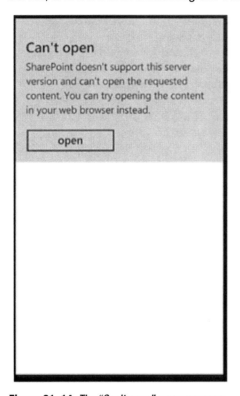

Figure 21–14. *The "Can't open" error message.*

Here are some things you can do to attempt to fix the problem:

- **Check the address**—This suggestion may sound simple (or even obvious), but the solution can actually be a bit more complex. While typos in the address can occur, you may also have entered `http://` instead of the `https://` that your company may require. Be sure to check the entire address for errors.

- **The SharePoint server isn't running SharePoint 2010**—Earlier in this chapter, we mentioned that your company's **SharePoint** server must be running **SharePoint 2010** for the **Office Hub** to be able to connect to it. If it isn't, you'll see the "Can't open" error, and you'll need to open the site in your web browser.

■ **You don't have the correct certificate files installed**—Some **SharePoint** servers may require that certain certificates be installed on your phone. Certificates are small *key* files that tell the server that your phone is allowed to connect. If you know your company is running **SharePoint 2010** and you still cannot connect, ask your system administrator if you need to install any certificate files on the device in order to connect. You can install these files by emailing them to yourself (or having your admin email them to you), and then opening these files as you would any other email attachment. You might also be able to go to a special website on your phone and download the certificate files from there (again, check with your IT support person). Once you download these files to your phone, you will be prompted to install them. At this point, you can attempt to connect to the **SharePoint** server again.

Resolving the "Can't Connect" Error

You may also encounter the "Can't connect" error when trying to connect to a **SharePoint** server. It will look something like the error shown in Figure 21–15.

Figure 21–15. *The "Can't connect" error message.*

Here are some things you can do to attempt to fix the problem:

- **Do nothing, hit retry**—Oddly enough, this worked quite frequently in my testing. So, before you try the following solutions, hit the **retry** button shown in Figure 21–15 once or twice.

- **Check your Internet connection**—Make sure you can browse to other websites, download email, and do other things that require an Internet connection.

- **The SharePoint Server isn't accessible on the Internet or your wireless network**—Your **SharePoint** server might not be available on the Internet or the wireless network you're connected to for security reasons. Try using a non-company-issued computer to connect to the server. If you still can't bring up the site, it's likely your system administrator has blocked traffic from either the Internet or non-corporate devices from accessing **SharePoint**. If your laptop requires you to log into a Virtual Private Network (VPN) before accessing **SharePoint**, then this is a good indication that the **SharePoint** server isn't accessible online. Windows Phone 7 currently does not support VPN connections.

I hope you're enjoying your **SharePoint** server connection and that you didn't even read this last section on troubleshooting! I also hope that you will find Windows Phone 7 to be a great way to stay in touch with your office while on the go!

Finally, I'd like to take a moment to thank Nuno Luz, a Microsoft MVP from www.pocketpt.net, for letting me connect to his **SharePoint** server. Without his help, this chapter would have been much more difficult to write!

Chapter 22

Using Maps

Many years ago—many being less than 10, in this case—the ability to access a map on the go meant investing in multiple books of maps that you kept in your car. Yes, you could plot directions on the Internet; however, if you were driving and found that I-76 was closed for three hours, you had no easy way to detour from Toledo to Richmond (not that I would know this from personal experience!).

But then came the marvel of GPS devices that could hold maps for the entire country. And now we can use our phones to look up, not only directions, but even what the area looks like and how the traffic is flowing in real-time. That's some pretty slick progress in less than 10 years. In this chapter, we'll take a trip through your Windows Phone 7 device's **Maps** application, exploring its many features and capabilities!

Getting Started: Opening Maps and Finding Your Location

Getting started with the Maps app is easy. Follow these steps to start the Maps program and find your current location:

1. Turn on and unlock your device.

2. Tap the **Arrow** icon in the upper right of the screen to access the **applications** list. Next, tap **Maps** (see Figure 22–1).

Figure 22-1. *Launching the **Maps** program.*

3. If this is the first time you've used **Maps**, you'll see a screen asking whether you will allow the app to use your current location (see Figure 22–2). While the **Maps** program will still function without your current location, you will find this program much more useful if it can access this information. Tap **allow** or **cancel** to continue.

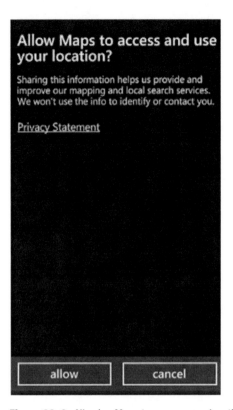

Allow Maps to access and use your location?

Sharing this information helps us provide and improve our mapping and local search services. We won't use the info to identify or contact you.

Privacy Statement

| allow | cancel |

Figure 22–2. *Allowing Maps to access your location.*

4. Once you start the **Maps** program, it will either attempt to zoom in on your current location (if you selected **allow** on the previous page), or it will show a map of the country (see Figure 22–3). You can use your fingers to move around the map; tapping the **Me** button returns you to the map that shows your current location.

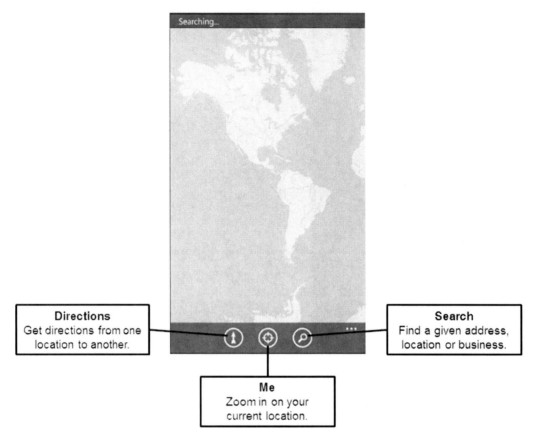

Figure 22–3. *The Maps interface.*

5. You can also double-tap the screen or "pinch" to zoom in on the map.

TIP: Pinching and stretching comes in handy in many apps and situations on your Windows Phone 7 device. You can *pinch* the screen by placing two fingers on the screen slightly apart (usually a thumb and forefinger) and then pulling them together. You can *stretch* the screen by placing two fingers on the screen and then moving them apart. In the **Maps** program, *pinching* zooms in on the map, while *stretching* zooms out.

Finding a Location and Getting Directions

Now that you know the basics of using maps, you're ready to dive into a real-world, practical example: finding a location and getting there. Let's assume you want plan a long-distance trip. Follow these steps to do so:

1. Follow the steps in the preceding section to open the **Maps** application.

2. Tap the **search** button (see Figure 22–3). A **Search** bar will appear.

Figure 22–4. *Searching for a location.*

3. Enter the intended destination of your long-distance trip. My own example uses a famous address in computer circles: Microsoft's main campus in Redmond, Washington (see Figure 22–4). Once you enter your search, press the **Arrow** key in the lower right.

4. If the **Map** program has trouble finding a location, it may prompt you with a few possibilities. You can tap one of these choices to confirm the location you originally wanted. If your address is fairly unambiguous (such as the one I entered), the **Map** program will show the location on your phone's screen (see Figure 22–5).

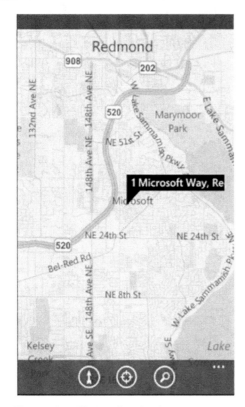

Figure 22–5. *The location pinpointed.*

5. The default zoom level shown in Figure 22–5 is a bit far out. As noted in the
    previous section, double-tapping or pinching the screen zooms in a bit more (see
    Figure 22–6). However, it still doesn't bring you in extremely close.

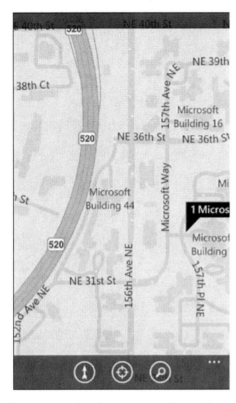

Figure 22–6. *Zooming in closer to the location.*

6. Let's say you want to know a bit more about the area of the country you plan to visit. Are there lots of pretty trees and mountains? Is there a desert? Are there many cars? Perhaps you can answer some of these questions by drilling down further on the map. To do so, keep zooming in until the map shows your preferred level of depth. Once you zoom in beyond a certain point, the **Maps** application switches to **aerial view** and shows you a satellite picture of the area. Figure 22–7 shows an aerial view of the address I entered previously: apparently, Redmond consists entirely of trees and funny-shaped buildings.

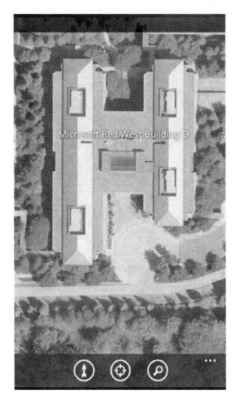

Figure 22–7. *Zooming in to see the satellite image.*

7. Before you embark on your trip, you might want to check the traffic, so you can find the best way to get out of town. Tap the **Me** button to get the **Maps** program to display your current location. Next, tap the **Ellipsis** button and then tap **show traffic**. You will now see the traffic around your current location. For example, Figure 22–8 shows the traffic around my office in New York City. A red line indicates the traffic isn't moving very fast at all, a yellow line indicates it's moving slightly faster, and a green line indicates clear sailing. Even at 7 PM on a Saturday, there is a bit of congestion around my office. Oh well, I still want to take my long roadtrip!

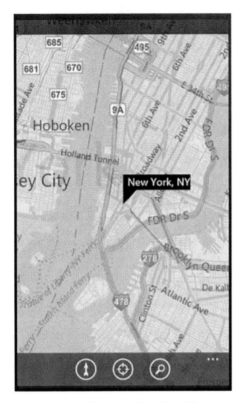

Figure 22-8. *Traffic around New York City.*

8. Next, tap the **directions** button (see Figure 22–3). By default, the **Maps** program will enter the last searched-for location in the **Start** field (in my case, New York), and your current location in the **End** field. If you find that your locations are mixed up (e.g., your **Start** location is listed as **End**) you can tap the small **Arrow** icon to the left of the word **End** to move that destination to the **Start** field (you can see this **Arrow** icon in Figure 22–9).

> **TIP:** Searching for a location doesn't necessarily mean you want directions on how to get there; you might just want to find information about that particular location. Tapping the **search** button, entering a query (e.g., "Steven's House of Knives"), and then hitting **search** will show you all of Steve's locations (or close matches) in the area. You can tap any of the name "bubbles" that appear to bring up details about a given location, including its address (which you might then plug into your car's GPS or give to a friend!).

Figure 22–9. *Switching locations.*

9. You enter your destination in the **End** field by typing the number 1. As you type, a drop down box will appear. This box shows recently searched-for locations that match the destination you're entering (see Figure 22–10). If you see your destination in this list, tap it. Otherwise, continue to enter the full address and continue on.

Figure 22-10. *Choosing a recently searched location for the destination.*

10. At this point, your phone will begin to search for directions (see Figure 22–11). This may take a few moments because the phone needs to look up the best route for you to take; it does so by contacting the servers for **Bing Maps**.

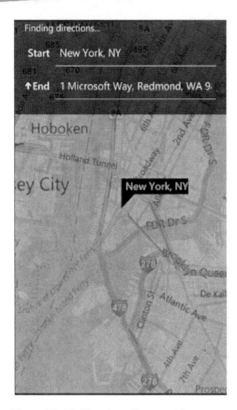

Figure 22–11. *Maps is routing your trip.*

11. Once your directions are set, you will see a list similar to the one shown in Figure 22–12. As you use your finger to move up and down the list, the map at the top will show the intersections of interest (see Figure 22–13).

Figure 22–12. *Showing turn-by-turn directions to your location.*

Figure 22–13. *Moving the map will also adjust the directions below to focus on the particular portion of the map being viewed.*

12. At any time, you can also tap outside the directions on the map to see a fullscreen version of the map (see Figure 22–14). To get back to the detailed directions, tap the **Ellipsis** key and choose **route details**.

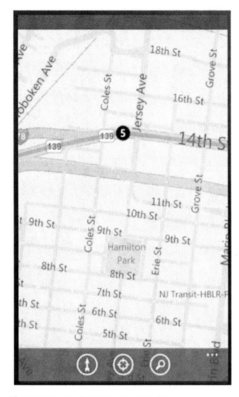

Figure 22–14. *Full screen map view.*

13. It wouldn't be practical in the scenario described, but let's imagine that at some point you decide to channel your inner Forrest Gump and walk from your current location to your destination. Figure 22–15 shows a small **Walking man** icon at the top of the screen. Tapping it asks **Maps** to provide you with walking versus driving directions.

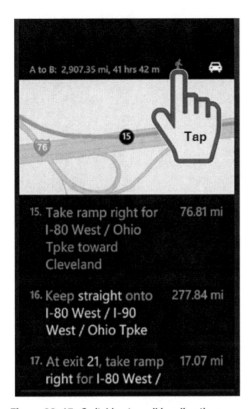

Figure 22–15. *Switching to walking directions.*

Certain locations cannot be mapped by walking, however (such as my NYC to Seattle trip). In such cases, you will get an error similar to the one shown in Figure 22–16.

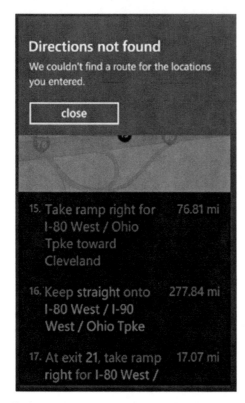

Figure 22–16. *Maps reporting that directions could not be found.*

There were some fanciful elements to the trip I laid out, I admit; however, the process of walking through these steps has taught you how to search for a location, get walking or driving directions, and much more.

Maps Settings and Menu Options

The preceding walkthroughs cover the most significant features of the Maps application; however, a few small details remain:

1. On the main **Maps** screen, tapping the **Ellipsis** button brings up more options (see Figure 22–17). For example, **Clear map** will let you clear the currently set destination; **Ariel view on** will let you turn on satellite imagery at any zoom level; and, as discussed previously in this chapter, **Show traffic** will show you current traffic conditions, if available. To see more options, press **settings.**

Figure 22–17. *Maps menu options.*

2. The settings for the **Maps** program (see Figure 22–18) let you turn on and off location use by the program. You can also delete historical information (e.g., searches you've made) from the **Maps** application by tapping **delete history**. For example, you might want to ensure that your ex's address never again pops up as you search for a new destination!

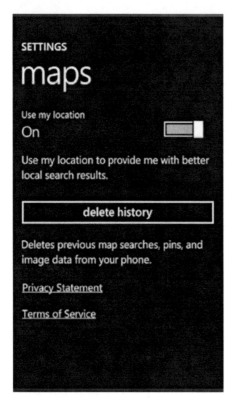

Figure 22–18. *Maps settings.*

As you've seen, the **Maps** application in Windows Phone 7 is extremely robust. Powered by Bing, this application will help you navigate to new locations, figure out where you are, and even tell you how long it might take you to get somewhere (a tip: if you're in New York City, budget at least an hour to get from anywhere to anywhere else)! The **Maps** program on your phone is much more convenient than using those giant old map books we all used to carry in our cars. It's also much easier to store properly than a 14-panel folding map!

Chapter 23

Connecting to the Zune Software

In November 2006, Microsoft launched Zune, a portable music and video player that provided a unique and fun way to listen to and watch media on the go. Along with the physical Zune devices, Microsoft also released the **Zune** software. This software enabled users to manage their media and connect with others, a feature Microsoft called *Zune Social*. Zune Social allows you to see what your friends are listening to, helping you to discover new music you might like.

While developing Windows Phone 7, Microsoft realized that the **Zune** software could serve as a logical way to manage music, movies, and pictures on your phone. So, it included a version of the **Zune** software on your Windows Phone 7 device that largely mimics the behavior of the aforementioned Zune devices. In this chapter, you'll learn how to listen to music and videos on your phone, as well as how to connect your phone to your computer and synchronize it with the **Zune** software.

Downloading and Installing Zune

To get started, you'll need to download and install the **Zune** software. These steps will walk you through that process:

1. On your computer, go to www.zune.net and click **Get the Zune software** (see Figure 23-1).

Figure 23-1. *Acquiring the Zune software.*

2. On the next page, you're given two options. First, you can create a new Zune account and download the software. Second, you can simply download the software without creating an account (see Figure 23–2). You may wish to create an account, so that you can use the social and music discovery features of Zune once you install the software. However, if you've already created a Zune account, you can simply download the software to your computer.

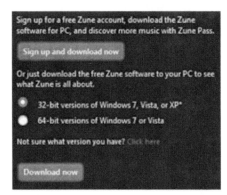

Figure 23–2. *The Zune download options; 32- and 64-bit downloads are available.*

TIP: Zune accounts are free; however, you may wish to sign up for a Zune Pass, which lets you pay a flat fee each month for access to all of the music in the Zune online store on a subscription basis. Additionally, you receive ten songs per month that you may download and keep, even if you cancel your Zune Pass later. If you're a heavy music listener and like discovering new albums and artists, this might be a good deal for you to look into!

3. Once you set up an account (or choose your operating system and click **Download**), the **Zune** software will begin downloading. To make sure you get the correct version, click the **Start** button on your computer, then right-click **computer** and choose **properties**. This screen will tell you what version of Windows you are running and whether it is 64-bit. The file is around 100 MB, so it may take awhile to download on slower connections. Once it downloads, double-click it to start the installation process.

NOTE: While Windows Phone 7 is designed to work best with the **Zune** software on a Windows PC, Mac users can use the Windows Phone 7 Connector for Mac to synchronize their phones, too. At the time of writing, the tool is still in Beta and doesn't have a full homepage—however, you can download it by using your favorite search engine and searching for "Windows Phone 7 Connector for Mac."

4. Follow the steps in the installation wizard to install the **Zune** software. The installation process is fairly straightforward, so all you should need to do is click **Next** a few times, and the software will be installed.

5. Once the software has been installed, you can double-click the **Zune** icon on your desktop to start it.

Exploring the Zune Software

The **Zune** software is designed to be easy to navigate. It organizes your music by artist, album, and song. It can also manage videos, pictures, and podcasts. The following steps walk you through using some of the software's features:

1. On your computer, double-click the **Zune** icon on your desktop to start the software. After a few moments, the **Splash** screen shown in Figure 23–3 will appear.

Figure 23–3. *The Zune **Splash** screen.*

2. The first time the software starts, it may take a few moments longer to load than is normally the case. This is because **Zune** begins by cataloging your music, videos, and pictures. Once the software starts, a screen similar to the one shown in Figure 23–4 will appear. I'll discuss each part of this screen, starting in the upper left and rotating clockwise.

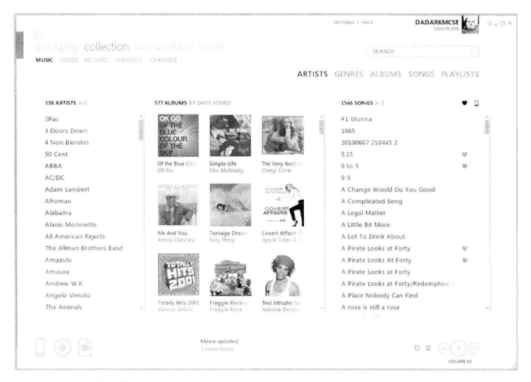

Figure 23–4. *The Zune **Music Collection** screen.*

3. Look in the upper left of this screen (see Figure 23–5). Clicking **Collection** highlights **Music** by default (Figure 23–5 details what each button does in this grouping). Click each item in the upper part of the bar to explore the **quickplay**, **marketplace**, and **social** options.

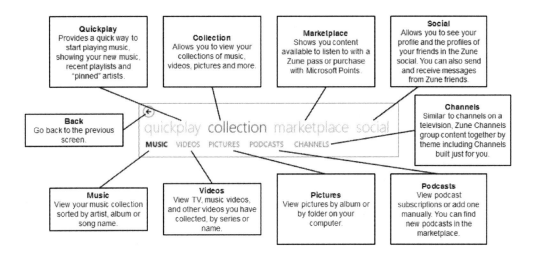

Figure 23–5. *Navigating Zune's options.*

4. In the upper right (see Figure 23–6), you'll find options to configure the software's **Settings** and access **help**. You'll also see your Zune profile picture and a **Search** box. The **Search** box will not only search your music and videos, but will also help you find items in the Marketplace.

Figure 23–6. *Searching for music in the Zune software.*

5. In the bottom right and center (see Figure 23–7), you'll see the current track you're playing, its progress, and a familiar set of buttons to control playback. Clicking the **Repeat** button will repeat the current playlist; clicking the **Shuffle** button will randomly play items in the list; clicking the **Previous**, **Play**, and **Next** buttons will let you control the track's playback; and clicking the **now playing** button will show the playlist with the album art in the background. The last option is perfect for displaying the music currently playing on a computer in a group setting, such as when at a party.

Figure 23–7. *Listening and controlling music.*

6. Finally, look in the lower-left corner of the screen (see Figure 23–8). You'll find icons representing your Zune device (whether it's an actual Zune player or your Windows Phone 7 device); a **Disc** button that represents a *burn* list, which is a list of music you wish to burn to a CD; and a **Playlist** icon, which you can use to drag-and-drop items onto a playlist from any screen.

Figure 23–8. *The* **Device**, **Disc** *(burn), and* **playlist** *buttons.*

7. The best way to learn about the **Zune** software is by playing with the different options and ways to view music, videos, and more. Once you're comfortable with the software, get ready to hook up your Windows Phone 7 device to your computer.

Connecting Your Windows Phone 7 Device to Zune

Listening to music on your computer is fine when you're at home. However, when you're on the go, it isn't really convenient to have your music on a computer—you want it near you on a device made for playing music, such as your Windows Phone 7 device.

> **NOTE:** If you have a previous version of the **Zune** software nstalled, you'll still need to update it to the most recent version before you can synchronize your phone with your computer. You can get the most recent version of the software at http://zune.net.

Follow these steps to connect your phone to the **Zune** software and leverage its ability to sync your music, videos, pictures, and podcasts:

1. On your PC, open the **Zune** software by clicking the **Zune** icon on the desktop.

2. Use the included micro-USB cord that came with your phone to plug your phone in to a free USB port on your computer.

3. When your computer sees the device, it should display a message similar to the one shown in Figure 23–9 as it installs the proper device drivers for your phone.

Figure 23–9. *Installing the appropriate device drivers.*

4. Once the installation is complete, a message similar to the one shown in Figure 23–10 will appear. At this point, the **Zune** software should begin detecting your phone and start the setup process.

Figure 23–10. *The device drivers have been installed.*

5. If you've set up a password lock on your phone, a screen similar to the one shown in Figure 23–11 will appear, asking you to unlock your phone. Take your phone, slide up the **Lock** screen image, and enter your password.

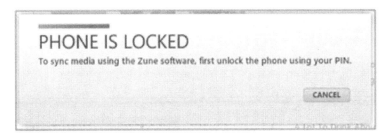

Figure 23–11. *Unlocking your phone.*

6. Once the phone is unlocked, the Zune software will begin the setup procedure, showing a screen similar to the one shown in Figure 23–12. Click **Next** to continue.

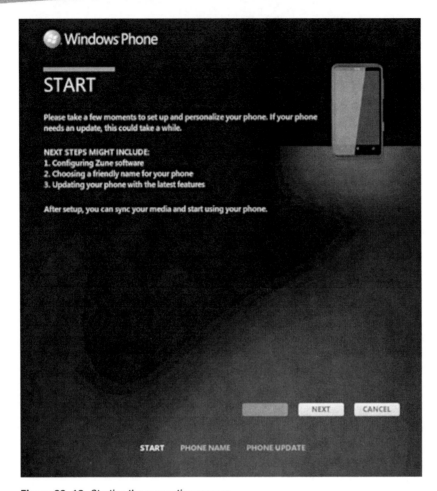

Figure 23–12. *Starting the connection process.*

7. Give your phone a meaningful name—such as "My Awesome Phone"—when you see the screen shown in Figure 23–13.

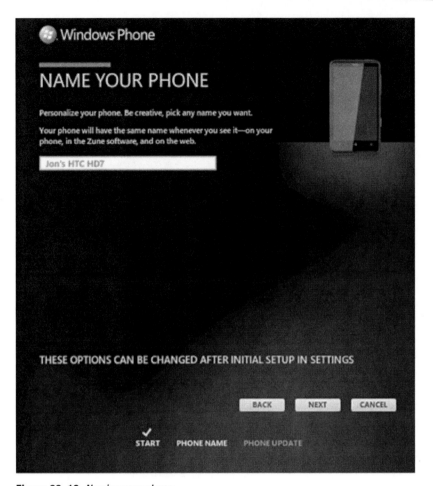

Figure 23–13. *Naming your phone.*

8. Next, your phone will go online and determine whether any system updates for your phone are available. We'll discuss updating your phone in more detail in Chapter 26: "Updating Your Phone"; however, if an update is available, you'll be able to walk through the process of updating your phone at this time. Once the update check is complete (see Figure 23–14), the setup process is done.

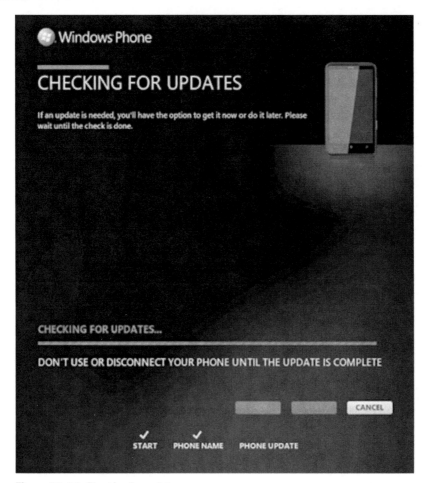

Figure 23–14. *Checking for updates.*

9. Once the setup process is complete, you'll see a **Summary** screen similar to the one shown in Figure 23–15. At this point, **Zune** will begin downloading any pictures you've taken on your device to your computer.

Figure 23–15. *Your phone's* **Summary** *screen.*

10. Once your photos are downloaded, you will be able to see them under the **Just added to collection** heading, as shown in Figure 23–16.

Figure 23–16. *Synchronizing content to your phone.*

11. Clicking the **View Sync Options** button shown in Figure 23–16 (beneath the **Last Sync** time) will bring up the **Sync Options** screen (see Figure 23–17). Clicking **All** or **Manually** under each media type (**Music**, **Videos**, **Pictures**, or **Podcasts**) tells **Zune** either to automatically upload all of a given content type—or none. The middle section, **Items I choose**, allows you to create sync groups for that media type, which you'll learn more about in the next section. Once you select your **Synchronization** settings and click **OK**, **Zune** will begin uploading content to your phone.

Figure 23–17. *Selecting what files should synchronize automatically.*

12. As the phone synchronizes, you'll see a screen similar to the one shown in Figure 23–18. Once the synchronization gets to 100%, your media is transferred, and you can begin using it on your phone.

Figure 23–18. *The completed synchronization process.*

Synchronizing With Sync Groups

Some of us have awesomely large music collections, or we rip all of our DVDs so that we can watch them wherever we are. This poses a problem because even the phones out today with the largest storage capacities might not be able to hold all our media files. Fortunately, the **Sync Groups** feature in the **Zune** software lets you configure exactly what you want synchronized to your Windows Phone 7 device:

1. In the **Zune** software, click the **Settings** button in the upper right.

2. Click **Phone** in the upper left of the screen (see Figure 23–19).

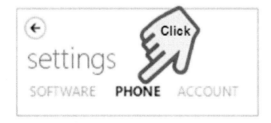

Figure 23–19. *Accessing your **Phone** settings in Zune.*

3. Click **Sync Groups** in the list of menu options to see a screen similar to the one shown in Figure 23–20. Click **New Group**.

Figure 23–20. *Creating a sync group.*

4. The **New Group** box will appear (see Figure 23–21). Customize this box so it contains whatever content you'd like. The setup I've shown will synchronize photos taken within the last 30 days to my phone. Remember that any content not set to **Items I choose** on the **Sync Options** page (see Figure 23–17) won't show up in the **Source** drop down box shown in Figure 23–21. This is because it's all or nothing for items in a sync group when it comes to syncing automatically.

Figure 23–21. *Configuring a sync group.*

5.   Click **OK** to enter the new group. The next time you synchronize, **Zune** will add the items to your phone.

> **NOTE:** When you specify **recently added**, the **Zune** software uses the date it added the photo to its library, not the time the photo was taken according to any information in the file (i.e., the EXIF information). This means that, when you first install the **Zune** software, the **Recently added** options won't be very useful until you've spent two to three months using the software because everything will be listed as **Recently added**.

Music, Videos, and Radio on Your Device

Once your device is loaded up with your music and videos, follow these steps to fire up **Zune** and listen to or view that media:

1.   Turn on and unlock your phone.

2.   Tap the **Music + Videos** live tile on your **Start** screen (see Figure 23–22).

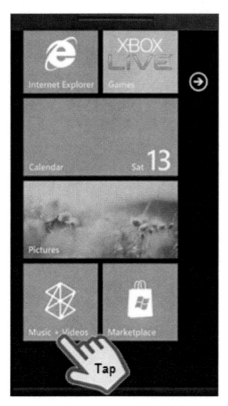

Figure 23–22. *The **Music + Videos** live tile which displays the last artist listened to.*

3. A screen similar to the one shown in Figure 23–23 will appear. From here, you can tap **music** to listen to the music you've uploaded, tap **videos** to watch videos, tap **podcasts** to view podcasts, and tap **radio** to listen to the FM radio included in your phone. You can also press and swipe to the right to see new items (see Figure 23–24).

Figure 23–23. *Navigating the* ***music + videos*** *interface.*

Figure 23–24. *New Zune content will appear here after you synchronize your phone.*

4.   In addition to listening to music you upload, you can also listen to music through the Zune Marketplace with your Zune Pass. (See Chapter 25: "Exploring the Marketplace" for more details on the Marketplace and streaming music.)

5.   To use the FM radio, you must first plug in headphones or you will receive an error (see Figure 23–25). As the error indicates, the headphones are required because your phone uses your headphones as an FM antenna.

Figure 23–25. *The* **No antenna** *error.*

6.   You can see the radio controls in Figure 23–26. These controls allow you to add your favorite frequencies and scan for stations by swiping your fingers left or right along the **Frequency** dial icon.

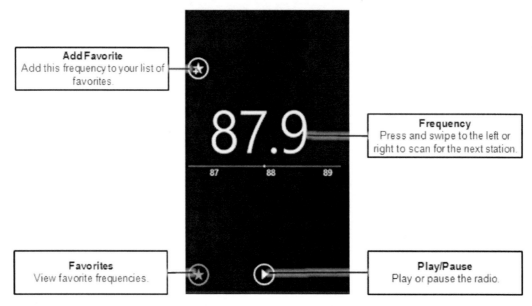

Figure 23-26. *Navigating the **FM Radio** interface.*

> **TIP:** The Windows Phone 7 radio tuner is RDS capable; if supported on your device, it will show information about the song and station you are listening to, so that you can download the song later in the Marketplace if you'd like!

Your Windows Phone 7 device is much more than a phone that can keep your life together. It can also *rock* in the sense that it can serve as your MP3 player, video player, any other media device you need. There are two great ways to learn about these options. First, you can follow the steps described in this chapter to explore everything described. Second, you can explore the various combinations of options available on your own to see where they lead you. The information provided in this chapter should give you a firm grasp of your phone's media interfaces and what they make possible, enabling you to set out on your own musical adventure.

Chapter 24

Using Your Phone With Xbox LIVE

Microsoft's Xbox 360 platform is one of the most popular console gaming systems in the world. As it created Windows Phone 7, Microsoft decided to take some of what makes the Xbox fun and exciting and put it right in the palm of your hand—by building a phone that could connect to Xbox LIVE to play games, check achievements, modify your avatar, and more. This chapter introduces you to the **Xbox LIVE** tile and highlights a few things you can do with it.

Accessing and Navigating the Xbox LIVE Tile

The **Xbox LIVE** tile is your starting point, not only for Xbox-connected gaming, but for any gaming on your Windows Phone 7 device (even non-Xbox games that you download through the Marketplace). Follow these steps to start exploring the **Xbox LIVE** tile:

1. Turn on and unlock your phone.

2. Tap the **Xbox LIVE** tile (see Figure 24–1).

Figure 24–1. *Accessing Xbox LIVE.*

3. Tapping this tile launches the **games collection** list (see Figure 24–2). This list will show you all of the games loaded on your device, as well as some games that you can try out by downloading them from the Marketplace (If featured on the Marketplace screens, these will be labeled "Try Now" on their icons, however this won't appear if you search for a game or see it in a list of applications).

Figure 24–2. *Xbox LIVE's **collection** pane.*

4. Pressing and sliding your finger from right to left reveals the **spotlight** list, from which you can find out about new Xbox games, services, and applications for your phone (see Figure 24–3).

Figure 24–3. *Xbox LIVE's **spotlight** pane.*

5. Pressing and sliding again brings up your Xbox avatar (see Figure 24–4), provided that you have added a Windows Live account connected to an Xbox gamertag already (see Chapters 1, "Setting up Your Phone / Initial Configuration", and 3, "Setting up Accounts" for more information on adding Windows Live accounts).

Figure 24–4. *Xbox LIVE's **Avatar** pane.*

6. Pressing and sliding once more brings up the **requests** list (see Figure 24–5). Requests refer to the system by which Xbox gamers can propose a game to other gamers (or "throw down a challenge," if you prefer). One of Windows Phone 7's most innovative features is the ability to play a turn-by-turn game (e.g., something like chess or checkers) with another person connected to Xbox LIVE anywhere in the world. The **requests** list lets you know if someone has invited you to play a game with her or if her turn has finished and you're able to make your next move.

Figure 24–5. *Xbox LIVE's requests pane.*

7. For a number of Xbox features, you'll need to install the **Xbox LIVE Extras** program, which we'll discuss in the next section. Before reading the next section, however, take a few moments and explore the menus you've just walked through to learn what goodies they hold!

Installing Xbox LIVE Extras

The **Xbox LIVE Extras** software was not included in your phone's pre-installed software; however, downloading and installing it is a breeze:

1. If the software is not installed, you'll be prompted to install it anytime you try to access a feature of the **Xbox LIVE** tile that requires it. One such feature is the **avatar** editor.

2. Follow Steps 1–5 in the preceding section. You should now see a screen that shows your Xbox LIVE avatar (see Figure 24–4).

3. Tap your avatar. You can tap anywhere on his body, although you should keep in mind he probably doesn't like being touched in the eye or nose, so perhaps just tap him on the shoulder or belly. (OK, I'm joking: your avatar *probably* won't care where you touch him.)

4. After a few moments, your phone will show you a screen similar to the one shown in Figure 24–6. Tap **install, allow**, and then **install** to start the installation process.

Figure 24–6. *Xbox LIVE Extra's listing in Marketplace.*

5. Once the installation is complete, you'll be able to proceed to the next section, where you can edit your Xbox LIVE avatar and view your accomplishments on your phone.

Modifying Your Avatar and Checking Achievements

Your Xbox LIVE avatar is your virtual self—and so you might want to keep him in style, perhaps by modifying his appearance. Follow these steps to modify your avatar:

1. Follow Steps 1–4 in the preceding section to install the **Xbox LIVE Extras** software. Once this is done, follow Steps 1–4 in the earlier "Accessing and Navigating the Xbox LIVE Tile" section to access your avatar.

2. Tap your avatar.

3. This brings up the **avatar** editor (see Figure 24–7). From here, you can tap your avatar and rotate it to see it from various angles; tap **change my style** or **change my features** to modify your avatar further.

Figure 24–7. *Editing your Xbox LIVE Avatar.*

4. When you're done making changes, hit the **Save** icon at the bottom. To discard your changes, hit the **Cancel** button.

5. A screen similar to the one shown in Figure 24–4 will appear; however, this time it will show your newly edited avatar. Now that your avatar is looking all snazzy, you might as well show off your achievements to all who care. Tap your most recent achievement to see a list of all achievements (see Figure 24–8). Tapping any of these achievements shows just how excited your avatar is to have made that achievement (see Figure 24–9)!

Figure 24–8. *Viewing Xbox LIVE achievements.*

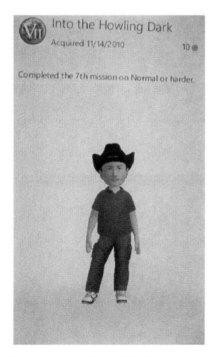

Figure 24–9. *An Xbox LIVE achievement displayed.*

A Few Final Notes

Obviously, this chapter can't cover all the possible games you can download and play; however, it can give you a sense of how to find games that may interest you (the **Xbox LIVE** tile), how to install any extra pieces the tile needs (e.g., the **Xbox LIVE Extras** software), and how to freshen up your avatar's style while on the go. To get the full experience of games on your Xbox, however, you should try some of the games highlighted in the various lists in the **Xbox LIVE** tile.

It may be that you would prefer for your games not to interact with **Xbox LIVE**. If so, you can disable the Xbox LIVE connection by going into your phone's settings and following these steps:

1. Tap the **Arrow** icon in the upper right to access the **applications list**.

2. Choose **settings**.

3. Swipe your finger from left to right to access **applications**, then choose **games**.

4. A screen similar to the one shown in Figure 24–10 will appear, and you can toggle the setting to **Off**.

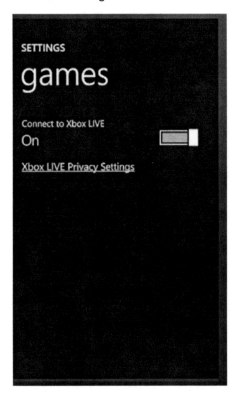

Figure 24–10. *Xbox LIVE Settings.*

The Xbox LIVE experience is best shared with a friend. So if you know someone else who has a Windows Phone 7 device, be sure to invite her to be your friend on Xbox LIVE and play a game. You might find the experience brings a bit of fun into your day when you'd otherwise have nothing to do!

Chapter 25

Exploring the Marketplace

Back in the Dark Ages (circa 2000), owning a device like your Windows Phone 7 phone (such devices were then known simply as PDAs) meant two things. First, it meant that you had your information with you wherever you went, as long as you synchronized manually by plugging into your computer regularly. Second, it meant that finding new applications and getting them onto your PDA could be a real pain. But now, 10 years later, things have changed dramatically: your information is generally stored online somewhere, and you can find all that cool stuff straight from your phone's screen using the Windows Phone 7 Marketplace. In this chapter, we will cover how to use the Marketplace to explore new applications, games, and music (From the Zune music store) that you can add to your phone. We will also discuss how to install applications, rate them, share them, and more!

Finding Applications and Installing Them

The Marketplace is filled with many interesting applications. It includes some free gems and a number of trial versions you can try out before you buy. Follow these steps to access the Marketplace:

1. Turn on and unlock your device.

2. Tap the **Marketplace** tile on the **Start** screen (see Figure 25–1).

Figure 25–1. *Accessing the Marketplace.*

3. A screen similar to the one shown in Figure 25–2 will appear. This screen will look slightly different, depending on which company makes your phone. First, the background may change to reflect featured applications. Second, it may include an entry above **apps** from your phone's manufacturer (e.g., the *Samsung Zone* or *HTC Apps*). These special areas let a phone's manufacturer add exclusive applications and content available only on that Windows Phone 7 device.

Apps
Tap here to find and install applications.

Games
Tap here to find and install games.

Music
Tap here to access the Zune marketplace, where you can buy music and videos.

Downloads
Tap here to show any pending downloads you have waiting.

Updates
Tap here to show applications with updates, which you can automatically download and install.

apps
games
music

2 downloads
3 updates

Figure 25–2. *The Marketplace main screen.*

> **NOTE:** Your phone may show that you have updates available at the bottom of the **Marketplace** screen (as seen in Figure 25–2). Tapping the update text (**3 updates** in this case) brings up a screen similar to the one shown in Figure 25–3. This screen lets you install free updates for all your applications at one time. It's generally best to be on a Wi-Fi connection when downloading apps and updates. While only some apps will *require* a Wi-Fi connection, all apps will certainly download faster over Wi-Fi than over a cellular data network.

Figure 25–3. *Viewing available updates for your apps.*

4. The screens in the Marketplace are all panoramas, which means you can swipe from right to left (or vice versa) to scroll between different areas. Let's flip through them quickly. Press your finger on the screen and swipe from right to left.

5. The next page shown (see Figure 25–4) displays featured items in the Marketplace, including applications, games, and music. Swipe once more from right to left.

Figure 25–4. *Featured marketplace content.*

6. The next page (see Figure 25–5) shows a specific featured application, game, artist, or album. Swipe once more from right to left to return to the main menu, and then tap **apps**.

Figure 25–5. *A featured artist.*

7. The **apps** menu opens to a featured application (see Figure 25–6). Swipe from right to left to go to the main **apps** menu. You can also continue to swipe right to left to cycle through other sections, such as **top** (the top selling items), **featured** (specifically featured items), and **new** (items recently added to the Market).

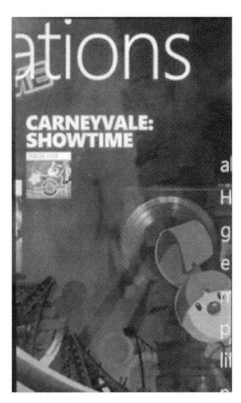

Figure 25–6. *A featured Xbox LIVE game.*

8. You should now be at the **apps** menu (see Figure 25–7). This menu shows the different categories of applications you might want to view. You can also search for applications by name by pressing the **search** button; you'll learn more about the **search** button in the "Finding Music and Videos" section.

Figure 25–7. *Viewing all categories.*

9. Now move down the list and open the **News and Weather** category; you'll see a screen that displays the top apps in this section (see Figure 25–8).

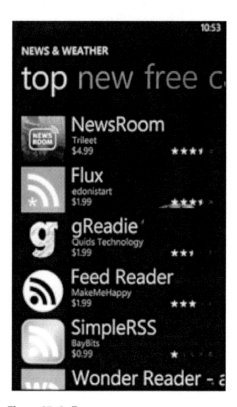

Figure 25–8. *Top apps.*

10. Like the previous two menus (**apps** and **marketplace**), this menu lets you swipe from right to left to see different views. One swipe shows you new applications (see Figure 25–9).

Figure 25–9. *New apps.*

11. A second swipe shows you the **Free categories** section (see Figure 25–10).

Figure 25–10. *Free apps.*

12. The top of the **Free categories** section shows one app that looks interesting: the official **Weather Channel** application. Tapping it brings up the app's information (see Figure 25–11).

Figure 25–11. *The Weather Channel app.*

13. The **Application information** screen contains a lot of information. First, it shows you the name, icon, and price of the application (free, in this case). You can also see a star rating that other users have entered, as well as a brief description. Moving the screen up with your finger also lets you view screenshots of the application, read the reviews, and find related applications that you might be interested in.

14. Tapping **install** will install the application (the button will read **buy** if the application requires you to pay for it or **trial** if you can install a trial version). If the application uses any special information on your device (such as your current location, as the Weather Channel does), your device will display a prompt and ask whether this is OK. You'll also be asked to confirm that you'd like to install the program.

NOTE: You can purchase applications, games, and music from your phone. If you do so, you'll need to either enter a credit card number or choose from a card previously on file with Microsoft (see Figure 25–12). In countries where Microsoft cannot accept credit cards, your purchase may also be added directly to your monthly cellular phone bill.

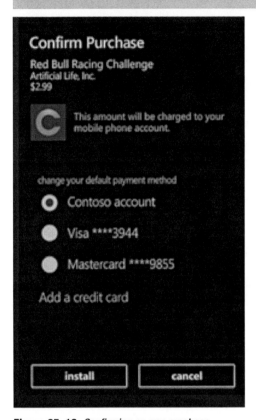

Figure 25–12. *Confirming an app purchase.*

15. Finally, you can tap **share**. This option sends the application's information to another person via email, allowing you to share a really cool application with your friends.

16. You can press the **Back** button to return to other parts of the Marketplace. You navigate throughout the rest of the Marketplace just as you do in the sections described thus far, so you should get the hang of it in no time. Later in this chapter, you'll also learn how to browse for applications from your desktop using the **Zune** software.

Uninstalling Applications

One of the great things about having the Marketplace on your phone is that it lets you explore a number of different applications. As you do this, however, you may find that these applications aren't exactly what you need, or you may find an app that does the job better. The good news: Uninstalling old application is very easy. Simply follow these steps to do so:

1. From the **Start** screen, tap the **Arrow** icon in the upper right to show the **applications** list.

2. Find the application you wish to uninstall. Press and hold until the pop-up menu appears. When it does, choose **uninstall**.

3. When the prompt appears asking whether you'd like to uninstall, choose **Yes**.

You can always reinstall an application from the Marketplace if you decide you'd like it back. If the application wasn't free (i.e., you paid for it), you will not have to pay again to re-download it to your device.

Finding Music and Videos

The **Zune** section of the Marketplace built into your phone operates very similarly to the **Applications** and **Games** sections discussed previously. However, it contains a few more features that you may want to explore. Follow these steps to learn about the **Zune** section, including how to search for music, videos, applications, and games:

1. Follow Steps 1–3 in the "Finding Applications and Installing Them" section to access the Marketplace.

2. Tap **music.** A screen similar to the one shown in Figure 25–13 will appear.

Figure 25–13. *A featured artist in the Zune music store..*

3. Pressing and swiping right to left or left to right will move through a variety of views, just as it did in the Marketplace sections discussed previously. You can see featured artists, new releases, and top albums. Figure 25–14 shows the **Genres** screen, which lets you explore artists and music by genre (see Figure 25–14).

Figure 25–14. *Different genres of music.*

4. While you can navigate through the **genre** menus to find one of your favorite artists, searching is usually faster. Press the **search** button on the front of your device to bring up the **Marketplace Search** screen (see Figure 25–15).

Figure 25–15. *Searching the Marketplace.*

5. Typing the name of the artist and pressing **search** causes the Marketplace to bring up a variety of possible matches (see Figure 25–16).

Figure 25–16. *Search results..*

6. Next, tap the name of the desired artist to see a list of that artist's albums (see Figure 25–17).

Figure 25–17. *Artist's album page.*

7. Swiping from right to left shows a list of songs (see Figure 25–18).

Figure 25-18. *Artist's song page.*

8. Swiping from right to left once more shows the artist's biography (see Figure 25-19).

Figure 25–19. *Artist biography.*

9. Now let's assume you want to hear a preview of one of the songs by that artist. Swipe back to the list of songs and press the small **Play** button beside a song name. The screen will change to show you the album cover and several controls for rewinding, fast forwarding, and pausing the song preview (see Figure 25–20).

Figure 25–20. *Previewing a song..*

10. You can also tap the **Volume** button on the side of the phone to access these controls (see Figure 25–21).

Figure 25–21. *The volume and music controls at the top of the screen..*

NOTE: If you are not subscribed to Microsoft's Zune Pass service, you can only listen to 30-second previews of the music in the Marketplace. If you sign up for Zune Pass, you can pay a low monthly rate ($14.99 a month at the time of writing) and stream as much music as you'd like through your phone or computer. You can also download a certain number of songs per month (10 at this time); these songs are included with your subscription. Of course, you can also use Zune Pass to stream all the music you'd like over your Internet connection.

As you can see, the **Zune** section of the Marketplace on your phone lets you find artists you're interested in, listen to their music, and learn more about them. If you really want to dig deeper though, you might find that exploring the Marketplace through your desktop computer makes it significantly easier to locate the perfect app, game, or song.

Using Zune Desktop Software to Discover Applications, Music, and Videos

The **Zune** software on your computer allows you to discover applications, music, games, and more. Follow these steps to use the **Zune** software on your desktop computer:

1. Open the **Zune** program on your computer. If you haven't already set up your phone to work with the **Zune** software, see Chapter 23, "Connecting to the Zune Software", for more information.

2. Click **marketplace** on the top bar to bring up a screen that shows featured and top artists and songs (see Figure 25–22).

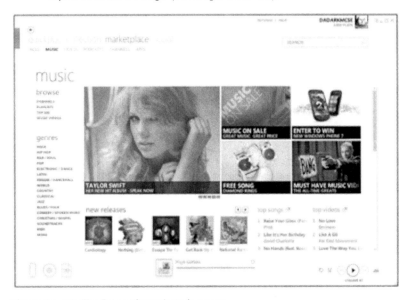

Figure 25–22. *The Zune software's main screen..*

3. Tapping the options in the top menu bar (see Figure 25–23) lets you cycle through customized recommendations (**picks**), **music**, **videos**, **podcasts**, **channels**, and **windows phone 7 applications (**apps).

Figure 25–23.*Navigating the Zune software's upper left menu options.*

4. You can also use the **Search** box in the upper right to search for any relevant items. For example, type in "weather channel" to see the results returned from such a search (see Figure 25–24). If your search terms bring up too many results to go through easily, you can click an item under the **Filter** list on the left to reduce the number of results.

Figure 25–24. *Searching in the Zune software..*

5. Clicking an application shows you the same information you would see on your phone; however, it may be easier to read all of this information on the bigger screen of your desktop computer. You can also rate an application here, as well as share your rating and opinion with others by clicking **view reviews** (see Figure 25–25) and then clicking **write review** (see Figure 25–26)..

Figure 25–25. *The Weather Channel application shown in the Zune Software.*

You can then enter your review using the **Message** box shown in Figure 25–27

Figure 25–26. *Reviews of the Weather Channel app.*

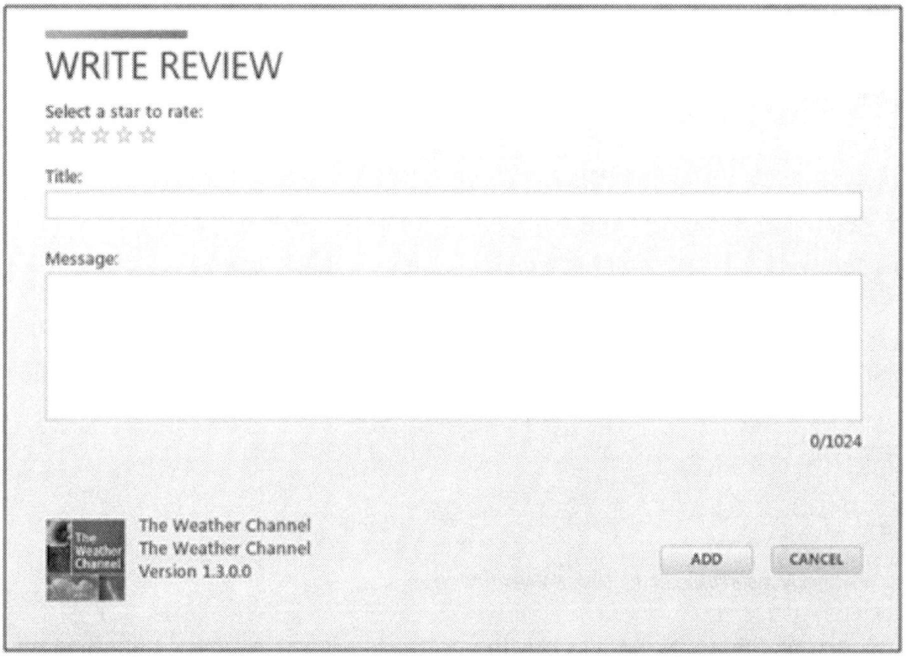

Figure 25–27. *Writing a review.*

> **NOTE:** You can also write reviews and rate applications on your phone. You can accomplish this in one of two ways. First, you can navigate to the **Product** page in the Marketplace by tapping **view reviews** and then entering text in the box at the top. Second, you can press and hold the entry for the application in the **applications** list, and then choosing **rate and review** from the pop-up box.

6. Finally, you can purchase applications for your Windows Phone device from your desktop computer. Let's assume that you find an application that you enjoyed using the trial version of; you can purchase the app by clicking the **buy** button. You will then see a **Confirmation** screen similar to the one shown in Figure 25–28.

Figure 25–28. *Confirming a purchase in the Zune Software.*

7. After confirming that you want to buy the app, you will see a screen informing you that the application will be installed (see Figure 25–29).

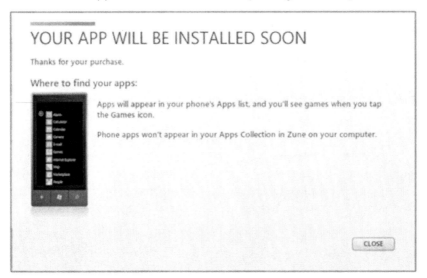

Figure 25–29. *App installation notification screen in the Zune Software.*

The Marketplace on your Windows Phone 7 device lets you find new applications, games, music, and more wherever you happen to be. Finally, accessing the Marketplace with the **Zune** software on your desktop enables you to find pretty much anything you need for your Windows Phone 7 device quickly and easily.

Chapter 26

Updating Your Phone

Windows Phone 7 is a full operating system, with a team of designers and programmers constantly working on new features, fixing bugs, and refining the software so that you get the best experience. However, these new features and fixes would mean nothing if there wasn't a way for you to update your phone to get the best possible experience. This chapter covers the Windows Phone 7 **update** feature, including how to check for an update and install it if one is available for your phone.

If you used a previous version of Windows Mobile, the predecessor to Windows Phone 7, you may have applied an update once or twice to your phone. While each update brought new features, it also wiped your phone, requiring you to re-install all of your applications and settings. Updates were also distributed through your wireless carrier, which meant that updates for two identical phones might be available months apart, simply because one was on Carrier A, while the other was on Carrier B. With Windows Phone 7, those two issues are eliminated. Updates no longer wipe the phone, and Microsoft is distributing the updates directly!

Before diving into the update process, I'd like to thank my friend and fellow Microsoft MVP, Jason Dunn, for providing many of the graphics used in this chapter. Jason recently wrote a piece on `www.windowsphonethoughts.com`, and these graphics were used in that piece, as well. At the time of this writing, there are no updates for my Windows Phone, so I wouldn't have any images to show you if it weren't for the images shared by Jason!

Why Update?

One of the things that I often hear from users is that they don't quite know why they should update their computers, phones, or anything else that has an update available. The old adage comes to mind: "If it ain't broke, done fix it."

If you're wondering why you should bother with updates to your phone, here are a few points to consider—and perhaps a compromise. First, new features aren't the sole reason for updating software—updates also fix problems found in older versions of software. At the least, these problems can be annoying; however, at the worst, these problems can cause your phone to lock up or make it vulnerable to attack by unsavory characters. Updating isn't just for fun; it's also to stay safe.

Second, updating poses no risk to your data. And with Windows Phone 7, updating is relatively painless. Just block out an hour or so one night to do perform the update, and you're set. There is no need to re-install software, nor are there any forgotten settings.

Third—and this along the lines of the second point—you don't need to install an update within the first 24 or 48 hours it's available. In fact, it might be a good idea to wait a day or two to make sure that the update doesn't suffer from significant bugs of its own (a rare occurrence). This gives the creators of the update a chance to stamp out such bugs by the time you perform an update. It also gives you a chance to see what new features are available by reading any of the Windows Phone websites on the Internet. We'll discuss those websites—and other resources—in the next chapter!

Checking for Updates

Windows Phone 7 makes it easy to check for updates—in fact, your phone will passively check for them if you allow it. It will do this by default; however, you can configure your phone's settings by following these steps:

1. Turn on and unlock your phone.

2. Press the **Arrow** icon in the upper right to access the **applications list** and tap **Settings** (see Figure 26–1).

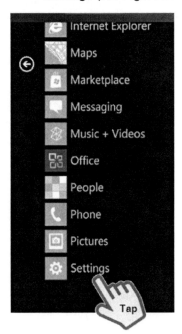

Figure 26–1. *Accessing **Settings** on your Windows Phone.*

3. Scroll down and tap **phone update** to access the update settings (see Figure 26–2).

Figure 26–2. *Accessing your phone's update settings.*

4. A screen similar to the one shown in Figure 26–3 will appear. This screen lets you decide whether to set your phone to notify you when an update is ready. You can also set whether the phone should use your cellular data connection to periodically check for updates. If you uncheck the second box, your phone will only check for updates when it has a Wi-Fi connection.

Figure 26–3. *The phone update settings when no update is available.*

5.   If an update is available for your phone, the screen will change to what's shown in Figure 26–4.

Figure 26–4. *The phone update settings when an update is available.*

6. If an update is available for your phone and you're not already on the **phone update** screen (which I doubt you'd venture into often for no particular reason!), you'll get a notification message similar to the one shown in Figure 26–5.

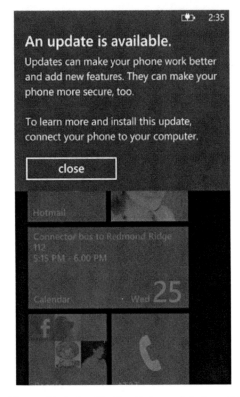

Figure 26–5. *A notification that an update is available.*

While updates are found and announced by your phone, the actual updating takes place using the **Zune** desktop software that we discussed in Chapter 23: "Connecting to the Zune Software." The next set of instructions assumes that you've set up your phone to connect to **Zune** (again, see Chapter 23) and are ready to install an update.

TIP: Updating your phone can take around an hour, so you'll want to plan ahead!

Installing a Windows Phone Update

As I mentioned at the end of the preceding section, Windows Phone updates are installed using the **Zune** desktop software. Follow these steps to install an update to your phone:

1. After plugging in your phone to your computer, you should receive a message regarding the update and asking whether you'd like to start the process. If you don't see such a message, click **settings** in the **Zune** software, then click **phone** in the upper left. On the list that appears, click **update** and the **Zune** software will manually check for updates and let you begin the update process.

2. The update process begins with an introductory **Update Your Phone** screen, as shown in Figure 26–6. This screen indicates that, while your phone is being updated, it cannot make or receive calls, so be sure you're not expecting anything important before you initiate the update process! This screen also gives an estimated completion time, although that depends a bit on how much data must be backed up on your phone during the update. And of course, it's not a good idea to disconnect your phone after you've initiated the update process.

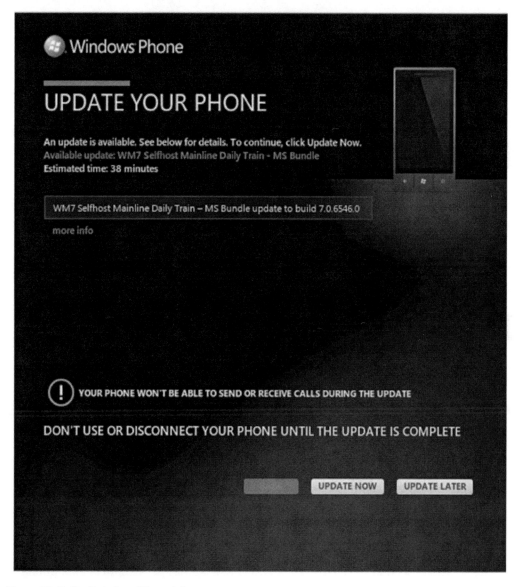

Figure 26–6. *The first step of the update process.*

3. Press **update now** to bring up the next screen (see Figure 26–7). At this point, your computer downloads the update package from Microsoft over your Internet connection.

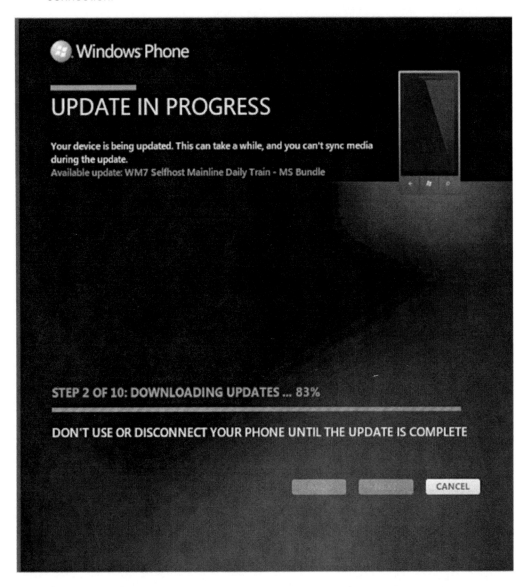

Figure 26–7. *The second step of the update process.*

4. Once the download is complete, the update is transferred to your phone (see Figure 26–8). This step transfers the update files to a special area of your phone; it doesn't modify your phone's software in any way.

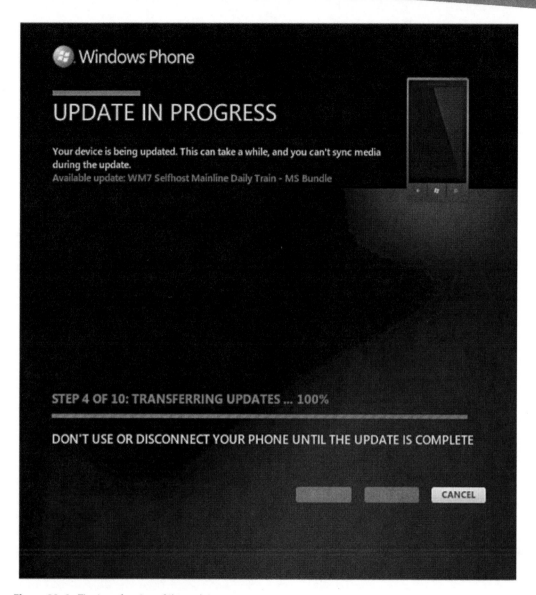

Figure 26–8. *The transfer step of the update process.*

5. The next screen (see Figure 26–9) is shown while the software prepares your phone for the update. The phone has to start up in a special **Update** mode; this part of the update process simply tidies up any loose ends on your phone and gets it ready to enter **Update** mode.

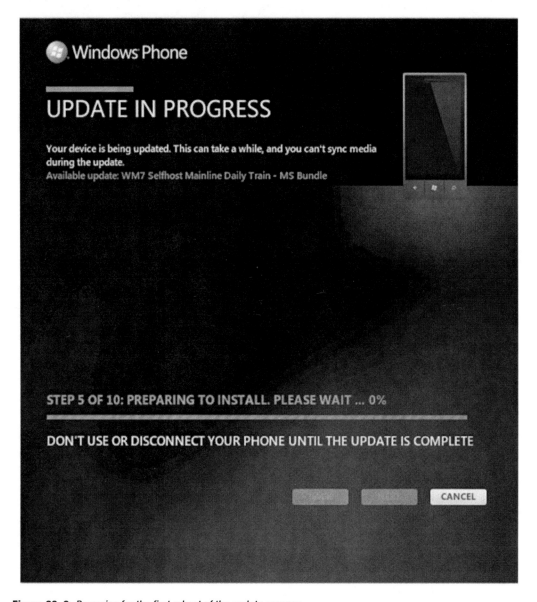

Figure 26–9. *Preparing for the first reboot of the update process.*

6. Next, your phone is rebooted into a special **Update** mode (see Figure 26–10). The screen on your phone may be different than what you typically see, and you cannot use it while it's in this mode. During this part of the update, you may see notification messages near your taskbar as your computer installs special drivers to communicate with the phone. This is normal.

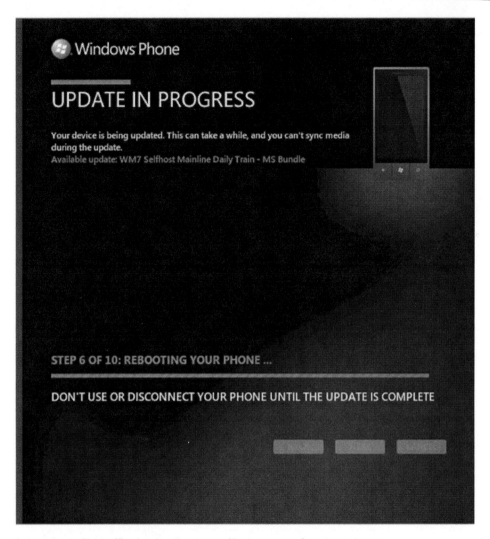

Figure 26-10. *The notification that the phone will reboot to continue the update.*

7. Once in **Update** mode, the **Zune** software makes a full backup of your phone (see Figure 26-11). This backup is insurance in the event that something happens during the update process (e.g., a power outage) that could possibly cause the update to stall out or need to be uninstalled due to a bug. One of the things that the Windows Phone 7 team was very adamant about to me and others is that the last thing it would ever want is for you to have a half-working phone due to an update being interrupted. Thus, the team implemented a full backup prior to updating your phone, just in case. The only downside is that this may take some time, depending on how much data you have on your phone.

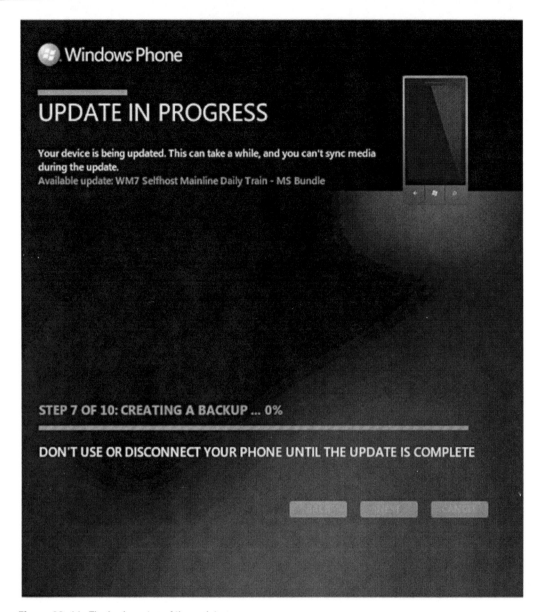

Figure 26–11. *The backup step of the update process.*

8. Once the backup is done, the update is installed (see Figure 26–12).

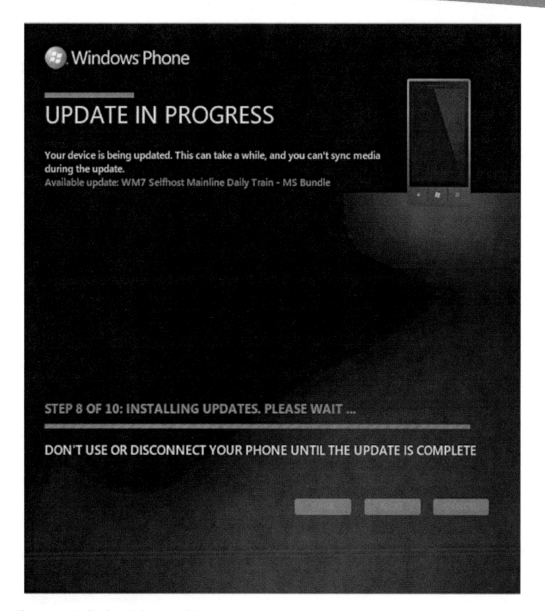

Figure 26–12. *The installation step of the update.*

9. Once the update is installed, the phone is booted back into its **Normal** mode (see Figure 26–13).

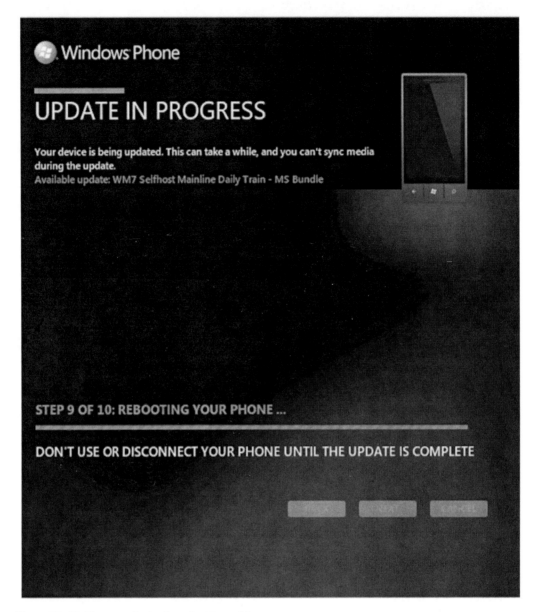

Figure 26–13. *The second reboot required for update.*

  10. After booting up again, the update package finalizes the update (see Figure 26–14).

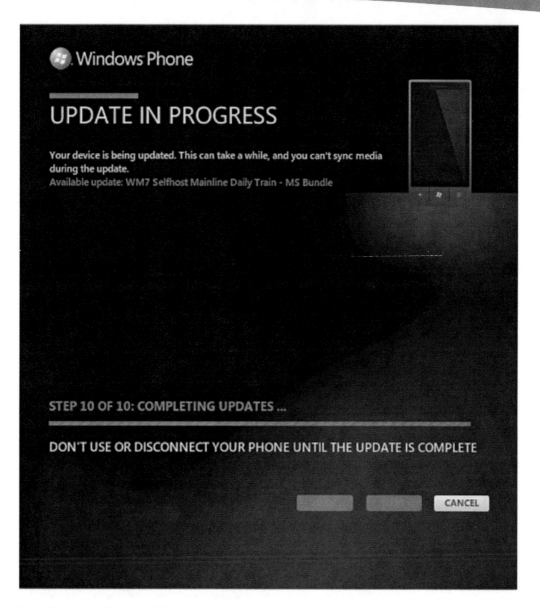

Figure 26–14. *The final step of the update process.*

11. When the update is done, you'll see a screen similar to the one shown in Figure 26–15. This screen lets you know that you can disconnect your phone and go back to using it normally. Your phone is now updated with the latest software from Microsoft; hopefully, it also includes some cool new features that you can explore!

Figure 26–15. *The update has been successfully installed.*

Now that the update is done, you'll be able to start enjoying the benefits of the fixes and changes Microsoft has made to your phone! You can also rest easier knowing that your data is always safe, even as the phone changes around it!

Chapter **27**

Resources to Explore

It's hard to believe we're already at the end of the book, isn't it? But even after reading everything in this book, you've only just started to explore what your Windows Phone 7 device can do. There are apps to download, music to listen to, games to play, emails to send, pages to browse, and more. And along the way, you'll probably want to check out different websites for information, reviews, and even help with specific questions. In this chapter, I'll point you to a variety of websites where you'll find tons of great information to help you continue on your Windows Phone journey!

Going Official—Help From Microsoft

The first place to go when looking for help is to the various websites Microsoft maintains for Windows Phone. An obvious place to start is www.windowsphone.com (see Figure 27–1).

Figure 27–1. *The Windows Phone website.*

This website includes a number of sections that cater both to those interested in Windows Phones and those who already own them. Since you're reading this book, I'm going to assume you probably already have a Windows Phone 7 device (or are close to purchasing one). Therefore, I'll focus on a few areas a Windows Phone 7 owner will probably find helpful. The first is the **Help and how-to** section, which you can get to by clicking **how-to** in the menu at the top (see Figure 27–2).

Figure 27–2. The **Help and how-to** section of the Windows Phone website.

The **Help and how-to** section provides a number of tips and tricks for both setting up your phone and using it to accomplish things you might not have thought of even after reading this book. It also answers a number of common questions and addresses some common concerns.

Another nice tool that Microsoft has made available is a quick-and-easy search that relies on the Bing search engine to help you find apps outside www.windowsphone.com. Simply go to www.bing.com and search for "Top Windows Phone 7 Apps." On the next page, click the **visual search** option (see Figure 27–3).

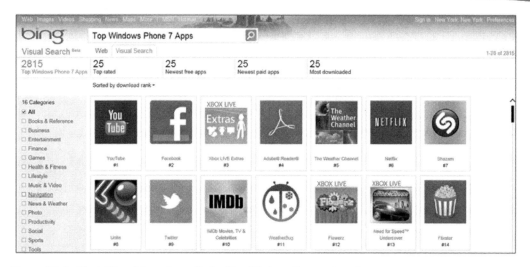

Figure 27-3. *Bing's* **Visual Search** *results for "Top Windows Phone 7 Apps."*

This should help you find apps you're interested in, even if you're not using your device at the time or near a computer with the **Zune** desktop software installed. It also shows you what's climbing the ranks of popular apps. If I haven't looked at the apps available in a month or so, I'm often surprised to find a host of popular new apps that I want to try!

But what if you encounter problems? Well, that's what the Windows Phone page on Microsoft Answers is for (see Figure 27-4). Head over to http://answers.microsoft.com/en-us/phone and click **Windows Phone 7**.

Figure 27-4. *The Microsoft Answers forum for Windows Phone 7.*

The Windows Phone 7 Answers forum is filled with knowledgeable experts who can help you get the most out of your phone. The moderators and Microsoft MVPs are clearly marked, and the forum is well moderated. This makes the site a safe and easy way to get help with your device. You can search the forums as well as read a list of common asked questions (Just look for the thread labeled "Windows Phone 7 Frequently Asked Questions" in the forum topic list, it should be near the top). In any event, no question is too simple, so feel free to jump in and post one. And hey, if you've got the time and desire, you can help out others by answering questions that you know!

> **NOTE:** This is probably a good time to discuss what a *Microsoft MVP* is. Microsoft gives its Most Valuable Professional (MVP) award to people in the community as a way of thanking them for leading user groups and helping others in online forums. The award is meant to recognize those who have taken the time (without compensation) to help users or help spread information regarding Microsoft products. MVPs are a diverse bunch of people that bring experience from a number of industries and professions to the advice they give. As you may find, veteran MVPs can be a source of great knowledge to users just starting out. On many Microsoft forums and even private websites, you'll see users proudly proclaiming their MVP status. You can find more information on the MVP program at http://mvp.support.microsoft.com.

Finally, Microsoft maintains a number of blogs regarding Windows Phone. It uses these blogs to announce new features and discuss how to get the most out of the device's existing features. You can find the Windows Phone blog at http://windowsteamblog.com/windows_phone/b/windowsphone/ (see Figure 27–5).

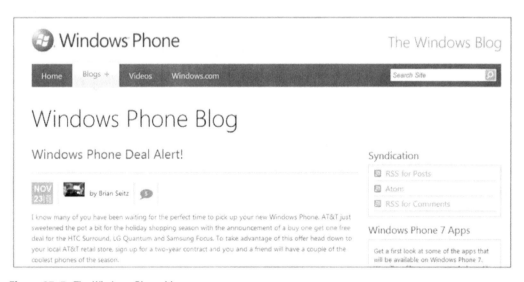

Figure 27–5. *The Windows Phone blog.*

Individual Websites, Forums, and Blogs

I've been writing and blogging about Windows Phone since 2005; and in that time, I've made quite a few friends within the blogging and writing communities. This section highlights some of their websites, which I believe you'll find useful as you explore your Windows Phone 7 device.

The first website—which I'm more than a little biased in favor of—is Windows Phone Thoughts (www.windowsphonethoughts.com). Originally called Pocket PC Thoughts, the site began as a blog by Jason Dunn, a Microsoft MVP since 1997 who began writing about what would become Windows Phone back in 2001. With a team of editors who have volunteered to serve an active community of forum users over the years, Windows Phone Thoughts features Windows Phone news, reviews, and commentary. I've been a regular contributor on the site since 2005, and I currently serve as the site's News Editor.

Other websites I'd recommend include (in alphabetical order):

- **BostonPocketPC**: Led by Windows Phone MVPs such as Steven Hughes (this book's technical reviewer) and Don Sorcinelli (a fairly devious fellow—in a good way, of course), Boston's Windows Phone user group home is full of information on meetings in the area features many posts about Windows Phone devices. This site is a must if you're in the Boston or New England area! Check it out at http://bostonpocketpc.com.

- **Gear Diary**: Judie Lipsett Stanford blows away the misconception that a woman can't be as into technology as a man—by being into it more than most men I know! Judie and her team review and discuss a wide range of gadgets and gizmos, as well as current tech news. Head over to http://geardiary.com.

- **MobilityMinded**: Johan van Mierlo and his group review and discuss all things mobile, including Windows Phone (of course!). Check it out at http://mobilityminded.com.

- **MoDaCo:** MoDaCo is always a great source for Windows Phone and other smartphone news. Visit it at http://modaco.com.

- **PocketNow:** A team of experienced editors keep PocketNow's content flowing. This site focuses on several smartphones, including Windows Phone, Google's Android, and Apple's iPhone. Visit the site at http://pocketnow.com.

- **wpcentral**: Dedicated exclusively to the Windows Phone and a member of the Smartphone Experts network, this site features news, reviews, and more. Check the site out at www.wpcentral.com.

User Groups

A final resource you might look into is a local user group. Windows Phone user groups are normally located in large cities (or regions) and led by volunteers who want to provide a place for people to meet and talk about Windows Phone devices. User groups can also serve as a great place to learn about new features for both end users and those writing programs for the phones. To find a user group near you, search the Web using Bing or another search engine. You can also ask in the forums on your favorite Windows Phone website or post a question on the Microsoft Answer forums. And if there isn't a group nearby, you can always start one yourself! In the New York area, a few fellow phone fans and I did precisely that last year, forming the New York Area Windows Phone User Group (NYPUG). To find out more about our group, visit our site at http://nypug.groups.live.com. You can find out more about the New England group at http://bostonpocketpc.com, or find out about groups in your area with a simple search.

Finally...

Learning a new piece of technology—even one as simple to use as a Windows Phone 7 device—can be daunting. However, in the end the best advice I can give is simply to find the best way for your phone to help you and go with that. If you really like using your phone just for email and phone calls, then don't worry about the music or apps. If you are a diehard gamer and find that's what you want to use your Windows Phone 7 device for, then so be it. And if you're just a regular person who wants a reliable and easy-to-use phone, just ignore the fancy stuff in Windows Phone 7 until you're ready. And when you are ready, I predict that learning to use those more advanced features will be fairly easy, given the consistent look-and-feel and form-and-function of the phone.

It's been a pleasure writing this book for you, and I hope that you've learned as much reading this book as I have writing it. And if you didn't get some of the cultural references in the screenshots, you can always ask me about them via email or twitter—I'm fairly easy to find. Thanks for reading!

Jon Westfall

http://jonwestfall.com
twitter: jonwestfall

Index

Time	What Jon Does With his Windows Phone 7	Learn more...
1:45 PM	**Listen to music** to help relax before presentation.	Connecting to the Zune Software—Ch. 23
2:30 PM	Get notification that a **phone update** is available for my Windows Phone 7. Make mental note to apply the update tomorrow!	Updating Your Phone—Ch. 26
3:45 PM	Almost time for my presentation, but my phone is missing! I'll send a **Ring** request to it so I can find it!	Managing and Securing Your Phone—Ch. 8.
5:15 PM	Presentation over, now I just need to enter my **notes** on how it went into OneNote Mobile!	Using Microsoft Mobile OneNote—Ch. 17
6:00 PM	Do a **search** about what alcoholic beverage is mixed into eggnog. Win office bet.	Searching your Phone & Using Speech—Ch. 9
7:00 PM	Finally home! Quickly change my Xbox LIVE avatar's clothing into something intimidating so my Utah friend knows I mean business tonight.	Using Your Phone with Xbox Live—Ch. 24
9:00 PM	After an hour of gaming, we take a break and I decide to **find out** what cool new tips, tricks, and apps are available for my Windows Phone 7.	Resources to Explore—Ch. 27
10:30 PM	Head to bed, put the phone on to charge. I get to sleep in tomorrow—so I decide to turn off the audible **email alerts** on my phone!	Customizing Your Phone—Ch. 6

Day in the Life of a Windows Phone 7 User

Wonder how your Windows Phone can play a role in your daily life from dawn till dusk (and beyond)? Check out this sample day, perhaps you'll find the area you want to know more about.

Time	What Jon Does With his Windows Phone 7	Learn more...
5:23 AM	The **Alarm** goes off, way too early, but hey, that's life!	Setting Alarms and Reminders—Ch. 11
5:30 AM	Lay in bed and check recent news both using **Internet Explorer** and a few **apps**.	Surfing the Web Using Internet Explorer—Ch. 14 & Exploring the Marketplace—Ch. 25
5:55 AM	Post **Facebook Status Update** that reads "Leaving for another wonderful day of work!"	Setting up Facebook and Twitter—Ch 5
6:10 AM	Arrive at Train Station. Scope out Traffic data in **Maps** to see the gridlock I'm missing out on.	Using Maps—Ch 18.
6:45 AM	**Review presentation** that I'm giving today on my phone, make a few small edits.	Using Microsoft Office Mobile PowerPoint—Ch. 20
7:45 AM	Get to office, put phone down but keep **Bluetooth headset** handy for calls. Also connect to office **Wi-Fi network.**	Setting up Bluetooth and Wi-Fi—Ch. 7
9:40 AM	In quick conversation with colleague, agree to meet next week on project. Check my **Calendar** and make a new entry for the meeting.	Using & Customizing the Calendar—Ch. 12.
11:45 AM	Send **text message** to friend in Utah, asking if he'd like to meet up for some Xbox gaming later today.	Using Text Messages—Ch. 13
12:10 PM	Check **email** while waiting for co-workers to join me for lunch.	Using Email—Ch. 4
12:20 PM	Make a quick **phone call** to said co-workers asking them where the heck they are!	Making Phone Calls—Ch. 2.
12:30 PM	**Take picture** of empty chairs around the table, to email to said tardy co-workers later.	Taking Pictures and Putting Them Online—Ch 15

Breinigsville, PA USA
04 February 2011
254807BV00002B/65-614/P